Mezcal in Oaxaca

Joe R. and Teresa Lozano Long Series
in Latin American and Latino Art and Culture

Mezcal in Oaxaca

A Craft Spirit for the Global Marketplace

Ronda L. Brulotte

University of Texas Press *Austin*

Printed in the United States of America
First edition, 2025

♾ The paper used in this book meets the minimum requirements of ANSI/NISO Z39.48-1992 (R1997) (Permanence of Paper).

Library of Congress Cataloging-in-Publication Data

Names: Brulotte, Ronda L., author.
Title: Mezcal in Oaxaca : a craft spirit for the global marketplace / Ronda L. Brulotte.
Description: First edition. | Austin : University of Texas Press, 2025. | Includes bibliographical references and index.
Identifiers: LCCN 2024029677 (print) | LCCN 2024029678 (ebook)
ISBN 978-1-4773-3095-1 (hardcover)
ISBN 978-1-4773-3096-8 (paperback)
ISBN 978-1-4773-3097-5 (pdf)
ISBN 978-1-4773-3098-2 (epub)
Subjects: LCSH: Mescal industry—Mexico—Oaxaca (State) | Mescal—Mexico—Oaxaca (State) | Mescal industry—Mexico—Oaxaca (State)—History. | Tequila industry—Mexico—Oaxaca (State)—History. | Handicraft industries—Mexico—Oaxaca (State) | Artisans—Mexico—Oaxaca (State) | Mescal—Marketing. | Food tourism—Mexico—Oaxaca (State) | Tourism—Anthropological aspects—Mexico—Oaxaca (State) | Tourists—Mexico—Oaxaca (State) | Women artisans—Mexico—Oaxaca (State)—Social conditions. | Mescal industry—Economic aspects—Mexico—Oaxaca (State)
Classification: LCC HD9393.6.M63 O29 2025 (print) | LCC HD9393.6.M63 (ebook) | DDC 338.7/63590097274—dc23/eng/20241118
LC record available at https://lccn.loc.gov/2024029677
LC ebook record available at https://lccn.loc.gov/2024029678

doi:10.7560/330951

"Have some wine," the March Hare said in an encouraging tone.

Alice looked all round the table, but there was nothing on it but tea. "I don't see any wine," she remarked.

"There isn't any," said the March Hare.

"Then it wasn't very civil of you to offer it," said Alice angrily.

"It wasn't very civil of you to sit down without being invited," said the March Hare.

—Lewis Carroll, *Alice's Adventures in Wonderland* (1865)

Contents

Illustrations

Maps

Figures

Preface

"Chupacabras—that's a great name for a beer!" exclaimed my colleague, delighted by the association with the Latin American folk creature who infamously attacked animals, sucking out their blood and leaving them for dead.

I was at La Biznaga with University of Arizona historian William "Bill" Beezley and several participants from his summer Graduate Field School in Modern Mexican History, which was held for many years in Oaxaca, Mexico. The restaurant was a popular destination for both locals and tourists seeking to eat and imbibe outside of the usual offerings. Even in 2011, Oaxaca had not yet exploded into the gastronomic hot spot it is today, and La Biznaga's menu—featuring ingredients such as dried hibiscus flowers, goat cheese, and dried cranberries sprinkled atop recognizably traditional Mexican fare—was both novel and refreshing.

Chupacabras, a Mexican craft beer, stood out on the menu among the usual Mexican beer suspects: Corona, Victoria, Indio, Dos XX, and Montejo. The provocative name and promise of something other than a typical lager-style beer was enough to convince me to try it. The American pale ale–style brew, produced by the Cupacá Brewery Company, far north in Mexicali, Baja California, had traveled nearly as far as I had to get to Oaxaca, a reminder of the artisanal brewing movement's extensive reach.

As our beers were delivered to the table, Bill mentioned that a friend and colleague of his at the University of Arizona, David Yetman, produced the Emmy Award–winning PBS series aptly named *In the Americas with David Yetman,* which featured a number of episodes based in Oaxaca.

He began describing his vision for an episode on craft beer, showcasing different microbreweries around the United States. As the daughter of fifth-generation hops farmers, I had some thoughts on the matter.

"You should go to the source. You really need to visit the Yakima Valley in Washington state, that's where most American hops are grown. Breweries are interesting, but most people have no idea about where the hops actually come from."[1]

I explained how the demand for craft beer had many hops farmers rethinking their market strategies. Back when I was a child, growing up in the 1970s and 1980s, most of our family farm's output was destined for Anheuser-Busch (maker of Budweiser) and Coors, which dominated the US beer market at the time. Home brewers in Chico, California, eventually launched Sierra Nevada Brewing Company in 1979, and a decade later the Boston Brewery opened, introducing Americans to its Samuel Adams brand. Nevertheless, while both were front-runners in creating consumer demand for craft beer, until the 1990s and even 2000s, most US consumers outside of home brewers and major urban centers had limited familiarity with beer other than national brands (e.g., Budweiser, Coors, and Miller) or mass-produced regional brands such as Pabst Blue Ribbon or Rolling Rock. In my home state of Washington, if you ordered a "local" beer at a bar, you would likely be served an Olympia or Rainier, neither of which would be considered a craft brew by today's standards. At the industry's low point in 1978, the United States counted fewer than one hundred breweries nationwide, with only forty-two brewery owners (Herz 2014).

Things would not stay this way. The microbrewing movement started to gather steam in the 1990s. And while the industry has experienced peaks and declines since then, the Brewers Association (n.d.) calculates that there were 9,709 breweries operating across the United States in 2022, compared to 2,670 just a decade earlier. These figures include large, non–craft breweries, but the overwhelming growth is among what the Brewers Association classifies as "regional craft breweries," "microbreweries," and "brewpubs." The burgeoning craft sector has decidedly shaped, and even changed, the number and types of hops grown. The new era of craft beer connoisseurship demands both novelty and variety. Case in point: whereas in my childhood my father would have grown the five or six hop varieties typical of the Pacific Northwest (e.g., Chinook and Cascade), today my sister, who has taken over the business to become one of the few women growers in the industry, is growing nearly sixty different varieties, including those that are gaining popularity in the craft brewing world (e.g., Bravo, Citra, and Mosaic). Recently, she even bred a new hop variety, cleverly named Bru-1, that has been sought out by craft brewers along the West Coast for its subtle pineapple notes.

"Craft beer—it's not unlike what's happening here in Oaxaca with mezcal," said Bill. "You should write your next book about that."

He flipped open the restaurant menu to show me an entire page of the various mezcals on offer. In addition to the unspecified *mezcal de la casa* (house mezcal), the list comprised mezcals differentiated not only by brand but also by region and agave type. This was not the first time I had heard of mezcal—a distilled agave spirit—but it was the first time I had noticed it prominently featured on a city menu in this manner, described with place of origin and agave varieties used.

Like so many products of arguably humble origins, mezcal, it seemed, had made its way onto the radar of tourists and tastemakers alike, not unlike the city of Oaxaca itself. It was clear that mezcal's introduction into the global foodscape would have profound impacts for those people and places within its orbit. At the same time, mezcal was a proxy for the type of place Oaxaca was becoming—a thriving food and arts destination that drew tourists from all over the world. And so, I decided to take my colleague's advice. I began laying the foundation for this project in 2011, allowing me to witness the mezcal industry's explosive growth over the course of a decade, which, depending on one's vantage point within the industry, may be a good or bad thing. And while I reserve judgment on this point, it is clear that mezcal's popularity is not about to fade any time soon. There is a popular Mexican saying that goes, "Para todo mal, mezcal, para todo bien, también," roughly translated to English as, "For everything bad, mezcal, and to celebrate all good as well." It may not be long before mezcal becomes a go-to drink—for good times and bad—for consumers not only in Mexico but around the world.

Mezcal in Oaxaca

Introduction | Mezcal Is Good to Think With

These days it seems that everyone is talking about mezcal in Oaxaca, Mexico, from locals who are discovering an affinity for the spirit to those who are seeking to profit in some way from its exploding popularity, two groups that frequently overlap. And it is not just in Oaxaca. Tastemakers in cosmopolitan locations around the world are just as important, if not more so, in creating the buzz. In 2010, the year most often linked to the mezcal boom, the *New York Times* food writer and critic Eric Asimov described mezcal as "the Next Big Thing" in the spirits world. He also inadvertently prophesized the writing of this book when he stated that "mezcal also allows us to examine how a spirit that has largely been made on an artisanal scale for local consumption comes to terms with global recognition."

Five years later, on the other side of the Atlantic, brothers Albert and Ferran Adrià, considered among the greatest chefs in the world, opened their twin Barcelona restaurants El Viejo Niño and Hoja Santa, serving up Mexican food inspired by their travels in Oaxaca, complete with a well-curated mezcal selection. Before his untimely death in 2018, the chef and author turned food celebrity Anthony Bourdain trekked to Oaxaca for his popular CNN series *Parts Unknown* (season 3, episode 4). There he joined American artist and founder of Del Maguey Mezcal Ron Cooper on the top of a pyramid at Monte Albán, Oaxaca's most famous archaeological site, where the two waxed poetic about mezcal's sacred place within local Indigenous cultures as well as its sublime alcoholic punch.

How long Mexican mezcal will remain in the limelight is anyone's guess. It certainly has become more commonplace. Eric Asimov revisited the mezcal trend in 2020 in his popular *New York Times* column, making the following observation:

> Looking back at the last time the spirits panel tasted mezcal, I was shocked to realize that almost a decade had passed. The flavors and the sense of discovery we experienced still seemed so fresh. . . . Yet so much has changed since that tasting in 2010. Back then, mezcal was described as "the next big thing." It finally arrived, and with such an impact that the trend authorities over at *New York* magazine recently deemed it passé, at least as a cocktail ingredient.

Even if certain tastemakers have now moved on in search of the next big thing, mezcal still occupies a prominent place in the spirits world. This is a dramatic change from twenty, even ten, years ago, when mezcal was yet still unknown to many food and beverage trend forecasters.

When I first lived and studied in Oaxaca City as an undergraduate student in 1995, mezcal was always available, but it was not something that foreigners, Mexicans from other regions, or even many Oaxaca City residents necessarily clamored to consume or sell. It seldom found its way into boutique stores, and even more rarely into upscale restaurants with multicourse tasting menus, themselves a scarcity at the time. The hip *mezcalerías,* entire bar establishments devoted to the drink that now dot the city's downtown, had yet to appear. Meanwhile, the alcoholic beverages served at the city elite's most important social events typically did not include mezcal. Rum, Scotch whisky (Johnnie Walker being a perennial favorite), brandy, and tequila were ever-present at fancy garden parties and elaborately catered weddings, but in the midnineties mezcal still could not wholly escape its class associations with the rural and working poor. Mezcal, despite the regional pride associated with it, seemed to have its time and place: rural village celebrations and decidedly unpretentious bars and cantinas.

In fact, my first encounter with mezcal in 1995 was not in the capital city of Oaxaca. Rather, it was at a wedding in Teotitlán del Valle (see map I.1), a Zapotec-speaking community famous for its woven wool rugs that today has become a foodie destination in its own right, thanks to a handful of restaurants and cooking schools catering to a mostly tourist clientele (Hyrciuk 2019). The fact that several of my fellow students and I were at this wedding in the first place might be viewed as an early indicator of the direction in which Oaxaca was heading, where the presence

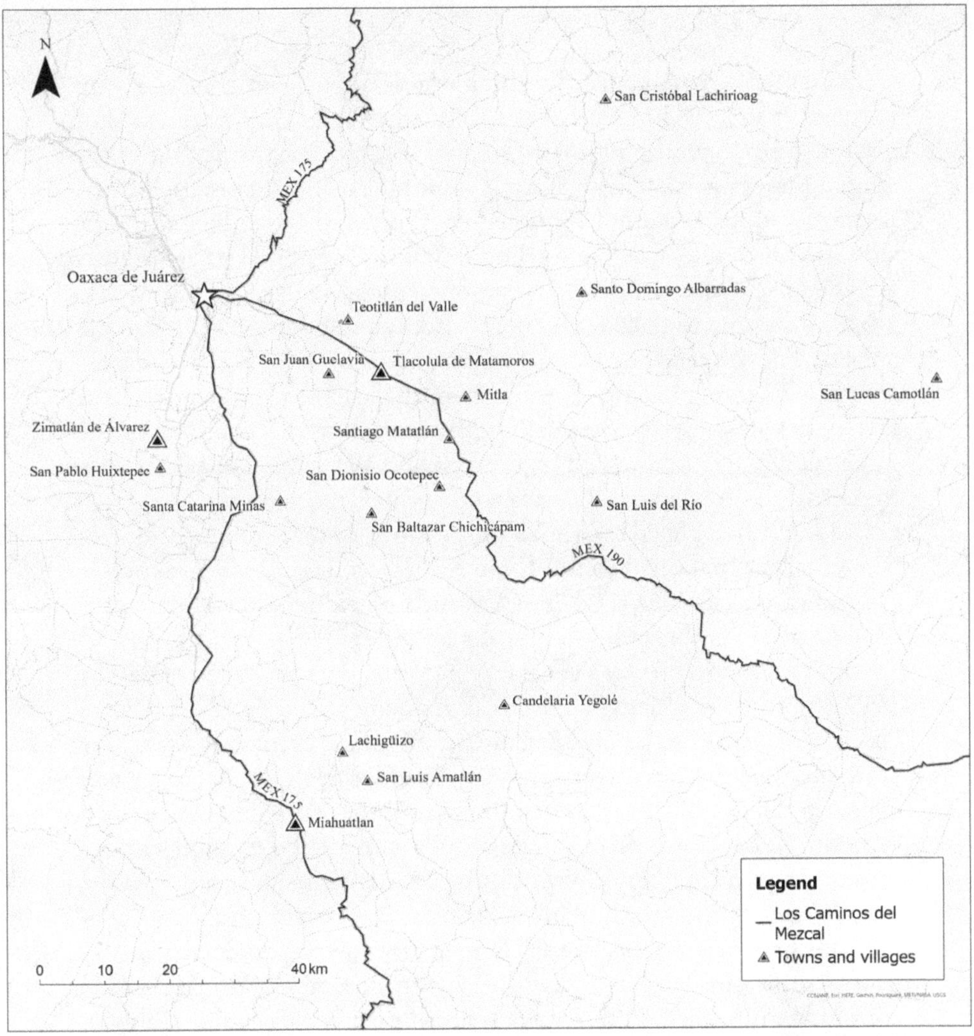

Map I.1 Map of Oaxaca indicating key locations named in the text. Map by Joseph Scala.

of outsiders expecting to participate in colorful, local celebrations was not only accepted but also becoming an industry in its own right.

It would be several years before I learned the local Spanish term *zocaleros,* given to the young, bohemian-looking men who roamed the central plaza (or zocalo), forming casual friendships and sometimes romantic relationships with female tourists. Suffice it to say that a female student in our group had become involved with one such young man, who, in an attempt to woo her, invited her and several friends, including me, to his cousin's wedding in the village.

I distinctly remember sitting on a wooden bench against a wall with two classmates, as an elderly man shuffled over to us, carrying a shot glass and a red, plastic jug—the kind of container many people in the United States associate with storing gas for a lawn mower in the garage. In ceremonious fashion, he studied each of us as we imbibed a hefty shot. I struggled to swallow the liquid that my untrained palate silently assigned to the category of "very smoky tequila" (a description I would eventually come to dislike the more I learned about mezcal). The man chuckled at the spectacle of us twentysomething drinking novices. He continued serving individual shots from the same little glass down the line of guests, only to eventually return, offering the contents of the same plastic jug. That would be my first and last direct encounter with mezcal until I returned to Oaxaca some years later, when I would again occasionally be obliged to drink a shot (or two or three) at a wedding or baptismal celebration in San Antonio Arrazola, an artisan community in Oaxaca's Central Valleys, where I conducted field research for my doctoral degree in anthropology in the early 2000s.

In addition to mezcal's centrality in local community festivities, by 1997 the spirit was being showcased annually at the Feria del Mezcal (Mezcal Fair) in Oaxaca City. Early iterations of the event were a far cry in scale and quality from the massive, pay-to-enter festival that today takes over two full city blocks of a downtown park. Indeed, when I attended it in 1998, the fair consisted of simple booths with attractive young women serving trays of miniature plastic cups of mezcal made from espadín, Oaxaca's most commonly domesticated agave variety, and sweet concoctions known as *cremas*, mezcal liqueurs that are flavored with various fruits, herbs, nuts, and dairy and that discerning mezcal drinkers today are quick to dismiss. With flavors such as piña colada, mocha, choco-banana, and strawberry, and a low alcohol volume (typically under 20 percent), *cremas* might seem to be the wine coolers of the mezcal world.[1] Ultimately, the only memorable mezcal was a *curado* (infusion) provocatively labeled "Viagra" that featured a mystery herb, branches and all, soaking in an amber-colored mezcal, which, as it turned out, made an amusing gag gift for a faculty member back home who had spent many years working in Oaxaca.

Today, not only is the world of mezcal much changed, it is fast evolving, as consumers across the globe develop tastes for diverse Mexican distillates that include not only mezcal, but also *raicilla*, *bacanora*, sotol, and a growing array of craft tequilas.[2] Indeed, a 2018 headline in *Forbes* magazine declared, "Forget Mezcal, Sotol Is Mexico's Hottest

New Spirit," underscoring the rapidity with which food and drinks come into and fall out of fashion (Japhe 2018). Yet in general, the renewed and growing interest in Mexican spirits does not seem poised to disappear any time soon. As long as the global appetite for artisanal products remains robust, mezcal's popularity seems unlikely to wane and, if anything, is likely to continue to rise. This means that mezcal will remain an important force in shaping the social and economic networks that bring the spirit to the world and, importantly, the world to Oaxaca.

Mezcal Basics

Before continuing any further, I should first clarify what is meant by the term *mezcal*. Somewhat confusingly, mezcal is used to refer both to any beverage distilled from agave *and* to a specific category of agave spirit regulated by Mexican federal law through its own denomination of origin (DO), a geographic indication similar to the French *appellation d'origine contrôlée* (AOC) used for wine and other agricultural products (Bowen and Valenzuela-Zapata 2009). Under the first definition, tequila is considered a type of mezcal, as are the other agave distillates mentioned above. Moreover, tequila possesses its own DO, implemented in 1974, specifying that it may be made from only one type of agave (*agave tequilana*, colloquially "blue agave"), with production geographically limited to the state of Jalisco and certain municipalities in four other Mexican states (Guanajuato, Michoacán, Nayarit, and Tamaulipas). While craft or artisanal tequila is undoubtedly enjoying a renaissance, much of the tequila consumed throughout the world is made in modern, industrial facilities (Valenzuela-Zapata and Nabhan 2004). This final point is particularly salient to the book's topic because mezcal as its own spirits category is so often constructed as a foil to mass-produced tequila in the contemporary marketplace.

This brings us to the second use of the term *mezcal*, and the way that it is generally used throughout the book. In 1994, the Mexican federal government established a DO for mezcal by publishing the Norma Oficial Mexicana NOM-070-SCFI-1994, turning mezcal into its own nationally protected beverage. For decades, all commercially sold mezcal was regulated by the Mexican Regulatory Council for Mezcal Quality (COMERCAM), a civil association formed in 1997 to enforce industry standards through its certification process.[3] In 2018, the Mexican Secretariat of Economy approved three private entities (Verification and

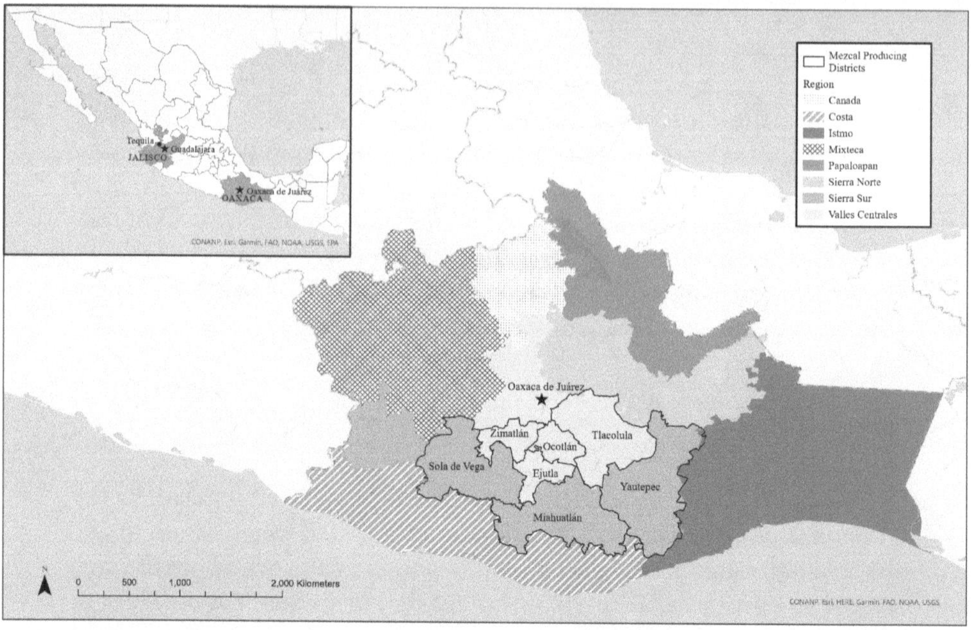

Map I.2 Oaxaca and its primary mezcal-producing districts. Inset map of Mexico denotes the states of Oaxaca and Jalisco. Map by Joseph Scala.

Certification PAMFA, Mexican Certification, and Center for Innovation and Agrifood Development of Michoacán) to assist in the mezcal certification process. Today, the bulk of mezcal comes from the southern state of Oaxaca, which accounts for upward of 90 percent of the spirit's total production (Arellano-Plaza et al. 2022). It is made in the districts of Tlacolula, Ocotlán, Ejutla, Sola de Vega, Miahuatlán, Yautepec, and Zimatlán (see map I.2). Oaxaca City, the state's geographic, political, and, most recently, tourist center is adjacent to several of these regions, making it the primary hub for much of the commercial activity involving mezcal.

But while mezcal has become synonymous with Oaxaca in many a consumer's mind, the DO for mezcal stipulates that it may also be produced in other Mexican states: Durango, Guanajuato, Guerrero, Michoacán, Puebla, San Luis Potosí, Tamaulipas, and Zacatecas. It also sets the amount of agave that the finished product must contain (100 percent), as well as standards related to how the agave is cooked, milled, fermented, and distilled (COMERCAM, n.d.). Unlike tequila, mezcal can be made from any number of agaves, including the widely cultivated espadín (*Agave angustifolia*), a species, incidentally, not endemic to the state of Oaxaca. Mezcal is also made from what are referred to as "rare," "semi-domesticated," and "wild" species, such as tepextate (*A. marmorata*), tobasiche (*A. karwinskii*), and tobalá (*A. potatorum*).[4] Notably, all these agaves take years to mature to the point at which they may be used to make mezcal, a minimum of four years, but more typically between eight and ten. An agave plant may be used only one time, for once it is harvested, the plant dies.

Apart from its geographic indication, mezcal is distinct from tequila in that it remains an overwhelmingly artisanal product, much of it produced in small family operations employing a handful of laborers, in which few, if any, production stages are mechanized (see figure I.1). In the most typical (if somewhat idealized) version of mezcal production, hand-harvested agave hearts are transported by truck (or domesticated animals in rough, mountainous terrain) to a small, rustic distillery. There they are chopped up into smaller pieces and then roasted in wood-fired, in-ground ovens for three to five days; it is this latter step of the process that imparts the smoky flavor associated with mezcal. Once the plant sugars have caramelized, the roasted hearts are then turned into a fermentable mash through nonmechanical means, either by human force using a wooden mallet or by an ox, horse, or donkey pulling a *tahona* (heavy stone wheel). The mash is then left to naturally ferment in wooden vats for up to a week, until it is ready to be distilled.[5] The most common types of stills used in Oaxaca are wood-fired copper or stainless steel alembic. Some producers use "Filipino" clay pot stills, which are believed to be an adaptation of clay stills historically used to produce a coconut spirit in the Philippines, a technology transported to Mexico via a colonial sea trade route. The final product will typically have an alcohol by volume (ABV) in the range of 40–55 percent and is ready to consume as an unaged mezcal, referred to in Spanish as *blanco* (clear) or *joven* (young). Less commonly, it may be aged for a period of time, resulting in either mezcal *reposado* ("rested" in oak for more than two months but less than a year) or *añejo* ("aged" in oak for over a year); these mezcals generally take on a golden or amber hue as well as what some consider to be softer, mellower flavors, much like an aged Scotch whisky. Mezcal may also be aged in glass vessels (*madurado en vidrio*) for more than twelve months, either buried underground or placed in a space with little fluctuation in light, temperature, and humidity. It is this laborious process that has earned mezcal the reputation as one of the most artisanal products in the world.

For the record, not all mezcal production conforms exactly to this model, as producers may look for ways to make the process more efficient. For example, some are now using mechanical shredders in place of mallets or *tahonas*, and I have seen what are essentially improvised steam ovens in place of wood-fired pit ovens to cook agave; I have also seen fermentation taking place in animal hides and, once, a repurposed washing machine tub. And there are always rumors floating about that such-and-such producer is using commercial yeast (even industrial fertilizer) to facilitate fermentation. Yet these deviations do not take away from the fact that mezcal is fundamentally a craft spirit. Of course industrially produced mezcal exists, but even the largest manufacturers in modern facilities, such as Benevá and Casa Armando Guillermo Prieto (both located just outside Oaxaca City), come nowhere close to the output of the biggest commercial tequila producers in Jalisco, such as José Cuervo and Sauza. To put it into perspective: in 2020 Mexico produced over 374 million liters of tequila but only 7.9 million liters of mezcal, as reported by the Tequila Regulatory Council (CRT) and COMERCAM, respectively. Sauza Tequila alone produced 639,000 nine-liter cases (5.6 million liters) in 2021.

Nevertheless, the mezcal market has demonstrated long-term growth, even in the face of a global pandemic (when disruptions to global supply chains were offset by increased alcohol consumption). COMERCAM (2024) reported that in 2023, Mexico produced 12.2 million liters of mezcal, with over half of that figure (7.8 million liters) exported abroad. While the United States is currently the world's largest consumer of mezcal, markets are expanding throughout the world; mezcal's 2018 entrance into the Chinese market, for example, points to one such area of growth. According to a market research report, the mezcal market was valued at US$242 million as of 2018, and projected to grow to US$738 million by 2027 (Transparency Market Research 2019). Notably, the increasing demand for mezcal in the United States is part of a larger trend in which consumers are opting for small-batch, craft spirits over large commercial brands (Dingwall 2021).

Thinking with Mezcal

Mezcal has a long history in Oaxaca, and Mexico more generally, and its rise in popularity has been accompanied by a growing body of scholarly literature as well as writings aimed at the wider public. The details of mezcal production are fascinating, and for those looking to learn more generally about the drink there are a number of English-language books that are a good introduction to the topic (De Barrios 2002; Janzen 2017; Lampert 2023; McEvoy 2014; Starkman 2021), in addition to compre-

Figure I.1 Harvesting cultivated agave by hand. Photo by author.

hensive online resources such as the Mezcalistas website (Mezcalistas, n.d.). Gary Paul Nabhan and David Suro Piñera's *Agave Spirits: The Past, Present, and Future of Mezcals* (2023) is a timely look at the industry and where it is headed, particularly in terms of sustainability. The numerous works by Sarah Bowen and Marie Sarita Gaytán cited throughout this book are essential reading for understanding mezcal and tequila in a sociological context. For those who read Spanish, a good place to start is the comprehensive volume *En lo ancestral hay futuro: del tequila, los mezcales y otros agaves* (Colunga-García Marín et al. 2007). There are also a number of excellent books that address everything from the drink's historical and cultural significance (Arellanes Meixueiro 1997; De Gortari and Escamilla 2009; Torrentera 2001, 2009, 2017; Valles Septién 1997; Vera Cortés and Fernández 2015) to the more technical aspects of its production (Sánchez López 2005). Mexican sociologist Domingo García Garza (2019, 2021, 2022) has written extensively in Spanish (and French) about the reinvention of mezcal as Mexico's national drink, including for the tourist market.

This book invariably touches on some of the same themes mentioned above. But it also invites the reader to consider mezcal as a microcosm of the ways in which everyday objects mediate complex global relationships. In 1962 French anthropologist Claude Lévi-Strauss declared food to be not only "good to eat" but also "good to think with." He believed that our everyday food practices, rituals, traditions, beliefs, and preferences had much to say about who we are and how we inhabit our material and social worlds. Some two decades later, the publication of Sidney W. Mintz's *Sweetness and Power: The Place of Sugar in Modern History* (1985) not only created a new focus of study within the discipline, the anthropology of food, it also made a compelling case for an individual food or commodity as an object of study. Since then, ethnographers have focused on single products, from the most mundane, such as broccoli (Fischer and Benson 2006), tea (Besky 2013), and rice (Davidson 2015), to what we have come to think of as gourmet or specialty foods, including artisanal cheese (Paxson 2012), quinoa (Seligmann 2022), and matsutake mushrooms (Tsing 2015). Though each of these foods may originate in or become identified with specific places (for instance, Darjeeling tea of India), they have the capacity to shed light on the often-overlooked corners of global capitalism. Meanwhile, human geographers have contributed to the conversation by looking at how food is constituted within spatial networks shaped by physical geography, culture, and economics (D. Bell and Valentine 1997; I. Cook 2004). Understandings of terroir and other place-based designations, in particular, owe much to the work of geographers, who have foregrounded questions of space, place, and power in their approach to food systems (e.g., Joassart-Marcelli and Bosco 2017; Sommers 2008). I draw significantly on both of these scholarly traditions through a focus on mezcal, a product that is highly place specific while at the same time evocative of the interconnectedness of people and place through an emerging global market.

Even though mezcal may not be considered critical to human biological survival in the same way as a food staple (although some may beg to differ), this book makes the case that it is certainly good to think with. The drink has evolved into many things in the twenty-first century marketplace, from a highly coveted craft commodity and marker of taste to a tourist attraction and a mechanism for rural economic development. On the one hand, mezcal is both a driver and manifestation of the growing desire for all things artisanal and, with it, a selective version of Indigeneity and rurality that Oaxaca is believed to represent; on the other, it is an exemplar of the way in which a once-campesino (peasant) or working-class food and drink is transformed into a celebrated elite or boutique product. Moreover, a closer look at these processes reveals the structural inequalities that enable them. As painful as it is for well-meaning consumers to confront such realities, this book is also premised on the idea that a full understanding of mezcal accounts for its less seemly side and, as such, touches on issues such as the consumerism, gentrification, migration, racism, and gender inequities underlying the drink's commercial success. This makes it a powerful lens through which to view the tremendous social and economic changes happening in Oaxaca, a place that has emerged as an epicenter of a voracious, elite consumer culture.

Importantly, many patterns identified here are not exclusive to mezcal or to Oaxaca. Geographer Michael Woods (2007) employs the term "global countryside" in writing about places where globalization is remaking rural localities, economies, and culture. The concept is useful because it "highlights the interconnectivity of rural localities in both the 'developed' and 'developing' worlds," while also recognizing that "the impact of globalization in rural localities is highly geographically uneven" (Woods 2007, 487). This intensification of rural-urban linkages is due to myriad factors that may include the development of commerce and new rural industries, migration, tourism, and improvements to physical and digital infrastructure. In this vein, one contribution of this book is to demonstrate how the mezcal boom has brought about a reappraisal of Oaxaca's rural sector. A place consigned to be another casualty of decades of neoliberal reforms—landscapes comprised of fallow fields and villages emptied out of working-age adults—has been selectively reimagined as a site for economic development built around increasing mezcal production for the new market. Indeed, the book posits Oaxacan mezcal as indicative of the "new rurality" that came to characterize Mexico and Latin America more generally during the second half of the twentieth century. Whereas older models of agrarian societies focused on primary economic activities related to agriculture, the new rurality accounts for the significant economic, demographic, and cultural shifts that have occurred in the rural sector, leading to greater integration with both local and global urban markets (Gaudin, Padilla Pérez, and Soloaga 2024).

The remaking of rural places has also reignited interest in craft products worldwide, with the countryside construed as a repository of so-called traditional objects and practices. The desire for handmade things, whether handicrafts or artisanal foods and beverages, is not new. Craftwork has cycled in and out of fashion since the late nineteenth century as part of a distinctly modern reaction to industrial produced goods. But the latest iteration of the "craft imaginary" (E. Bell, Dacin, and Toraldo 2021) has certain features that distinguish it from other historical moments in craft's popularity. Moreover, it may be considered part of the phenomenon of "enrichment" that sociologists Luc Boltanski and Arnaud Esquerre (2020) argue has characterized Western capitalism since the last quarter of the twentieth century. The enrichment economy is marked "both by deindustrialization and by an increased exploitation of certain resources that, without being entirely new, have taken on unprecedented importance." In this economy, the *past* is the foundation on which new markets rest, as enrichment is "based less on the production of new things than on an effort to enrich things that already exist, especially by associating them with narratives" (quoted in Diaz-Bone 2023, 18). The authors identify the arts and other cultural realms as those ripest for economic exploitation, and they specifically mention the trade in antiquities and contemporary art objects, the creation of foundations and museums, high-end gastronomy and luxury food, fashion, heritage creation, and tourism. It is not coincidence, then, that many of these same cultural industries surface in the book: they are deeply implicated in mezcal's own marketplace narrative.

Methods

I began the fieldwork for this project in 2011, thanks to a research leave that allowed me to spend five months in Oaxaca. Having done fieldwork in the region since 1998, I was already well acquainted with Oaxaca City and the surrounding Central Valleys and was able to quickly identify individuals, communities, institutions, and organizations that would be key sources of information on mezcal. As important as it was to gather information and contacts during my stay, one hallmark of ethnographic fieldwork, participant observation, was also vital to understanding what all went into the finished product. This became especially important the more I came to see mezcal as an extension of Oaxaca's craft culture. I was lucky that a close friend was working at a Tlacolula *palenque,* the Oaxacan name for a mezcal distillery. With his introduction, the owner permitted me to spend long periods of time on-site between 2011 and 2012, during which time I directly observed or participated in nearly all aspects of production.

An oft-heard lament in the mezcal world is that most consumers have no idea about the vast amount of work and knowledge that goes into producing a single bottle of mezcal. Spend a day doing any of the labor-intensive steps associated with mezcal-making, and this statement rings truer than ever before. Through participant observation I learned about the tools and the labor of agave harvesting, deeply skilled physical work that, with the exception of the trucks used to haul out the cut agave hearts (referred to in Spanish as *piñas*), is largely nonmechanized. Once the hearts were cut, I helped load and unload thousands of pounds of the plant (one time nearly crushing my leg), both from the truck that transported it from the field and, later, into the in-ground pit oven where it was roasted to a sweet, caramelized state. I found out that this was only the beginning of the process, which next entailed crushing the cooked agave using a horse-pulled *tahona*, a two-ton volcanic stone. I helped clean and fill oak fermentation vats (repurposed wine vats from France), shadowed an employee in charge of the distillation process, and joined a small assembly line—made up of three Indigenous Zapotec women from the nearby town of San Bartolomé Quialana—to bottle the finished product. We stood together for hours dipping each bottle neck in a signature coat of hot wax, allowing it to artfully drip down the sides, before the bottles were boxed and loaded on pallets destined for Texas.

In previous work, I focused on craft economies and the production of *artesanías*, or folk art, for Oaxaca's tourist market. Specifically, I traced the development of the global market for the brightly painted wood carvings now widely known as *alebrijes* in relation to a parallel souvenir trade in archaeological replicas at the UNESCO World Heritage site of Monte Albán (Brulotte 2012). I considered how archaeological replicas and wood carvings are positioned within a material-semiotic field, linked as much to one another as to the people who create and are shaped by them—even as their reception has diverged, with the archaeological replicas often maligned or disregarded as folk arts in their own right. One reason for this, I found, was that these replicas did not fit within an idealized version of Oaxaca. In other words, their "fakeness" is anathema to the cultural and historical authenticity Oaxaca has come to signify in the global marketplace.

The more immersed I became in the world of mezcal, the more I realized that it shared much in common with the folk arts that had captured my attention during my first time living in Oaxaca, in 1995, and that had kept me returning ever since. Apparently, I was not the first person to make this connection. In his insightful exposé of what he calls the "mezcal rush," author Granville E. Greene (2017, 180) recounts hearing mezcal described by others as "drinkable folk art." Yet I do not propose the comparison just because, as Greene points out, both are so-called traditional, handmade Mexican products. As I illustrate throughout this book, both *artesanías* and mezcal are central characters in the story of Oaxaca's evolution: from a once-wealthy colonial center to a geographically isolated, socioeconomic backwater to, in its most recent phase, a tourist mecca renowned for its art and gastronomy. Mezcal is not just "craft." It is part of a much-wider constellation of craft products, producers, consumers, and distributors, linking Oaxaca in both predictable and less visible ways to peoples and places all around the world.

With this framework in mind, I returned to Oaxaca to expand my knowledge beyond the agave fields and distillery. Between 2011 and 2018, I spent nearly twenty-four months doing fieldwork. This consisted of stays of a few weeks up to several months at a time, as well as an uninterrupted period of eight months in 2015. Though there is no universally agreed-on date marking the start of the mezcal boom, it is generally placed around 2010. This means that the time frame for my research coincided with an unprecedented rise in mezcal's popularity among US consumers. It also means that changes in the mezcal market since 2018 may not be fully reflected here. Nevertheless, my hope is that the book manages to give the reader a sense of the recent historical moment that marked the drink's transformation from international obscurity to acclaim.

Mezcal's spread across the United States was rapid but far from even. Like many gastronomic trends, it first took root in cities with robust bar and restaurant scenes, particularly along the East and West Coasts. Few, if any, of my New Mexico friends and colleagues had ever heard of mezcal back in 2011. The locally owned, boutique liquor store in my hometown of Albuquerque offered only a bottle or two of Del Maguey (more on this brand later), nearly crowded off the shelf by the ample tequila selection; when I asked the owner how often he sold a bottle, he estimated one or two every six months. Today, although Albuquerque is still not an epicenter of the US mezcal boom—that honor goes to bigger, tastemaking cities such as Los Angeles, San Francisco, and New York—mezcal crops up on cocktail menus around town, and local buyers may now select from brands other than Del Maguey. Across the years that I carried out fieldwork for this project, according to data from COMERCAM, mezcal production increased from 980,375 liters to 5,089,667 liters, and the number of brands for export from 68 to 240 (Lira, Robson, and Klooster 2022).

The mezcal I once only encountered situationally in Oaxaca was suddenly everywhere, the subject of books, blogs, food magazines, newspaper columns, and even the in-flight magazine on one of my many trips to Oaxaca on a US airline. A trip to visit friends in Austin, Texas, included a meetup at a local venue that coincidentally was a tasting room for the mezcal produced by the same Tlacolula distillery where I had unloaded my first freshly cut agave heart. Even though I am not one for slogans, I found myself agreeing with Del Maguey founder Ron Cooper's trademarked phrase "You don't find mezcal, mezcal finds you."[6] Mezcal's new public profile carried implications for how to actually study the drink. The *palenque,* the site of production most directly associated with mezcal-making, was an obvious starting point, but it represented only one node in a multidirectional process that not only brings mezcal to the consumer, but, increasingly, brings the consumer to the mezcal.

Understanding mezcal and its complex global connections thus required more than participant observation at the site of production. The information presented here is also the result of nearly nine years of formal interviews and informal conversations, as well as participation in guided tours, public tastings and talks, and workshops targeting audiences ranging from mezcal producers to mezcal consumers. For example, on one occasion I accompanied state government representatives on revitalization-driven visits to remote parts of the rural economic region known as the Mixteca (plagued by deforestation, out-migration, and, perhaps less widely known, drug trafficking); on another, I participated in a mezcal "boot camp" in the Sierra Norte region, where curious visitors from the United States camped out at a *palenque* and learned firsthand how to make *mezcal de pechuga,* a type of mezcal typically made for the holidays or special celebrations that is distilled with a chicken or turkey breast and often fruits and spices. This book is the ethnographic sum total of these experiences. It aims not to provide a comprehensive account of the mezcal industry but instead to examine emerging themes related to mezcal's transformation into a global product.

Book Overview

Chapter 1 examines how two of Mexico's homegrown agave distillates, tequila and mezcal, took divergent paths as a result of the country's colonial history and its legacy. In contrast with tequila, which developed national and international commercial markets beginning in the late nineteenth century, mezcal was not popularized outside of Mexico until the late twentieth century. Up until this time, because it was associated with Oaxaca, one of the poorest, most Indigenous states in Mexico, it was considered a drink of rural and working-class communities. But even though attitudes toward Oaxaca and its mezcal have flipped in recent decades, this chapter contends that this newfound popularity has created ownership of place and product in a way that mirrors the colonial order.

Chapter 2 examines how mezcal has taken its place alongside Oaxaca's many other craft industries. On the one hand, there is a tendency to see "craft" through a nostalgic lens, as processes and products rooted in the past; on the other, craft is at the vanguard of twenty-first-century design aesthetics and global tastes. Mezcal embodies this tension. This chapter thus discusses mezcal as part of a new craft imaginary and, by extension, Oaxaca as a place that has become a sort of shorthand for the idea of craft itself.

Chapter 3 looks at how mezcal's success in the marketplace is tied to the cultivation of a taste for the drink among non-Oaxacan consumers. It shows how the symbolic and material practices associated with connoisseurship of other foods and beverages serve as frameworks for making mezcal relatable or legible to outsiders. Such interdiscursive practices of taste, however, are bound up in social hierarchies that may contribute to mezcal's rarefied image.

Mezcal's meteoric rise in popularity has coincided with Oaxaca's growing recognition as a global culinary hot spot where authentic, Indigenous tradition is perceived to meld seamlessly with cutting-edge culinary innovation. Chapter 4 focuses on the development of mezcal tourism as a companion to Oaxaca's exploding gastronomic scene. Unlike tequila tourism in Jalisco, mezcal tourism was initially driven by chefs, bartenders, and others within the culinary industries. While the profile of mezcal tourists has broadened, the sector still depends on visitors who possess certain consumption skills and technologies. This chapter argues that they have played a decisive role in shaping not only the ways in which mezcal tourism is enacted, but Oaxaca's evolution into a particular sort of tourist destination.

Chapter 5 examines how gender divisions operate in the still-male-dominated world of mezcal production. The mezcal boom ushered in a new era in which women began to achieve visibility as both entrepreneurs and producers, which, from one perspective, may be seen as a significant gain from previous eras, when mezcal was considered strictly men's work. Nevertheless, the chapter draws attention to how gender difference may be strategically used to create value for the product without conferring material benefits for some women along mezcal's value chain. It raises the issue of whether a truly feminist politics is possible when free-market feminism is the order of the day.

Chapter 6 takes up the idea of mezcal as an economic panacea for a dwindling rural sector. There has been much speculation in the popular media and elsewhere that the opportunities created by the mezcal industry may be key to stemming out-migration from rural communities. Using ethnographic case studies, I argue that this line of thinking relies on an oversimplification of a much more complex rural reality. Not only have the ways in which people making a living in the countryside changed, mobility itself may play a role in achieving success within the mezcal industry back home. The chapter also points to the much-overlooked dynamic by which mezcal creates its own internal migration patterns and economic inequalities.

In the writing of this book, I have come to see mezcal as a palimpsest, an ephemeral object that contains "layered, contested, and evolving meanings" (Colwell 2022, 129). Thus, no single account of mezcal can account for what the drink has meant economically, culturally, and politically to the diverse peoples who have consumed it since colonial times. Yet all of these traces remain, as mezcal continues to develop as both a commercial product and an ideological container.

1 | Mezcal and Coloniality

> They earn more than they deserve to and then do not spend it on property or dowries for their daughters, but rather, on alcoholic drink, whether Castilian wine, or worse, something called pulque, a foul-smelling, foul-tasting wine that they make from agave. This pulque makes them drunk and senseless faster and more violently than wine from grapes, and the more that we prohibit it, the more they insist on consuming it.
>
> —Francisco Cervantes de Salazar, *Crónica de la Nueva España* (circa 1560), translated by John Charles Chasteen (2016)

Writing about New Spain, later to become Mexico, Spanish philosopher and chronicler Francisco Cervantes de Salazar penned a patently negative commentary on local drinking habits: not only did he disapprove of the excessive drinking of the (presumably Indigenous) local people, but he also objected to their choice of intoxicant. Cervantes de Salazar, who would become one of the first professors at the Royal and Pontifical University of Mexico (a precursor to the National Autonomous University of Mexico), would be neither the first nor the last to cast dispersion on pulque, an alcoholic drink derived from fermented agave sap that was made in Mexico long before the arrival of the Spanish. On the contrary, his comments reflect the pervasiveness of narratives by colonial Spanish and criollo writers linking the degenerate nature of Native peoples to alcohol consumption throughout the Americas (Earle 2008). Never mind that the "foul-smelling" pulque was not any stronger than the fruit-based wines, and certainly less so than the various distilled alcohols, introduced and enjoyed by the Spanish; or that overindulgence in alcoholic beverages was not unique to Indigenous communities. Alcohol consumption—both how much and what kind—was one of many historical lines separating the so-called civilized from the barbaric, the colonizer from the colonized in Mexico. Mezcal's status as an alcoholic drink was invariably defined by the same colonial order. Like pulque, mezcal, a drink conceived in the so-called New World, would never be accorded the same preferential status as Old World wine and brandy.

Yet for all the disdain Mexican elites expressed toward agave-based alcohol from the colonial period onward, these drinks were, historically, important cultural elements in many small Oaxacan towns, Indigenous and mestizo (or racially "mixed") alike, where they played an integral part in ritual and communal events such as baptisms, weddings, funerals, and Catholic saint day celebrations. Mezcal was and still is used to bless agricultural plantings and harvests as well as inaugurate new homes and other community works. It also figures predominantly among the offerings families make to their deceased loved ones during the Day of the Dead celebration each fall. It is safe to say that for most of its history, mezcal was more prominent in local markets than in national, and certainly global, ones. In contrast with Mexico's other well-known agave distillate, tequila, which developed national and international commercial markets beginning in the late nineteenth century, mezcal was not widely popularized outside of Mexico until the 1990s (Gaytán 2014; Huerta Rosas and Luna Zamora 2015; Orozco 2014). As such, mezcal has long been associated with Oaxaca, one of the poorest states in Mexico, as a drink of Indigenous, rural, and working-class communities. Even as it has risen in popularity, mezcal, along with pulque, has still had to contend with the stigma of being a low-quality drink. Like with other so-called bootleg or backyard alcohol, represented by moonshine in the United States and *aguardiente* in many places in Latin America,[1] the idea that mezcal could potentially induce illness, even death, if not properly made is still prevalent, if less pronounced due to growing education on the subject.[2]

Early in my fieldwork, I heard mezcal referred to in English as "Mexican moonshine" or, more unflatteringly, as "gut rot," the implication being that imbibing it carried physical consequences beyond the garden-variety hangover. Later, while doing fieldwork in Oaxaca, I stopped in at a downtown city store to purchase a Spanish-language book titled *Mezcal: Elixir de larga vida*, which translates into English as "Mezcal: Elixir of long life" (Arellanes Meixueiro 1997). The woman who managed the store, an acquaintance, walked me over to the register to ring up my purchase. She snorted when she read the title. "¿Larga vida? Más como elixir de la muerte rápida!" (Long life? More like the elixir of a quick death!). The woman, who was married to a rug weaver from the Indigenous Zapotec community of Teotitlán del Valle, said she was all too familiar with the ill effects of alcoholism. She went on to explain that several members of her large extended family struggled with the disease—a sober reminder that despite all the celebratory buzz around mezcal in recent years, Mexico has a long, complicated history with the drink.

It is perhaps not so surprising that few agricultural substances have been so historically divisive as alcohol. Scholarly work on the subject must therefore contend not only with alcohol's geographic and social pervasiveness throughout Mexico, and Latin America more widely, but with these conflicting positions surrounding it. Alcohol is at the center of daily and ritual life in many communities throughout Mexico, but it has also been a destructive force both physically and socioeconomically (Brandes 2002; Eber 2000; Mitchell 2004; W. Taylor 1979; Toner 2015). Should alcohol be considered alongside other foods as a substance that fosters commensality and the expression of group identities, or should it be seen as one among many drugs whose deleterious effects have made them subject to intense public scrutiny, regulation, and even prohibition? A summary look at the role of alcohol throughout Mexico and Latin America more broadly tells us that both questions are of historical and continuing relevance (Pierce and Toxqui 2014).

Comestibles, or food and drink, have a been cornerstone of empire-building as well as the maintenance of social divisions throughout human history (Laudan 2015). Within this category, alcohol has a special status as a psychoactive drug. Few who have downed a shot of mezcal would disagree that it produces a very different effect on the human body than does, say, a corn tortilla. And it is precisely this potent ability to alter physical and mental states that has made alcohol a marker of social status and boundaries par excellence in Mexico. From pre-Hispanic times to the present, alcohol consumption—how much, what type, and in what context—has been one way to distinguish ancient elites from commoners, Indigenous or Afro-descended peoples from European-identified ones, the urban poor from the urban elite, and men from women. Societies throughout the world have gone to great lengths to regulate and control alcohol production and consumption. In the Americas this resulted in conflicting and ambivalent attitudes toward alcohol. The sociality and community created through drinking were often undermined by its negative physiological effects, with drunken or unruly populations seen as potential threats to the socioeconomic order (Brulotte 2017).

Alcohol production, commercialization, and consumption have never been independent of the broader socioeconomic dynamics of Mexican colonialism and its aftermath (Mitchell 2004; Toner 2015). This means that race, class, and gender politics, which took on a nationalist tenor after the Mexican Revolution in the early twentieth century, have always played a role in how agave-based alcoholic drinks are differentiated and accorded value in the marketplace (Gaytán 2013). Sociologist Marie Sarita Gaytán (2014) has detailed tequila's ascension to

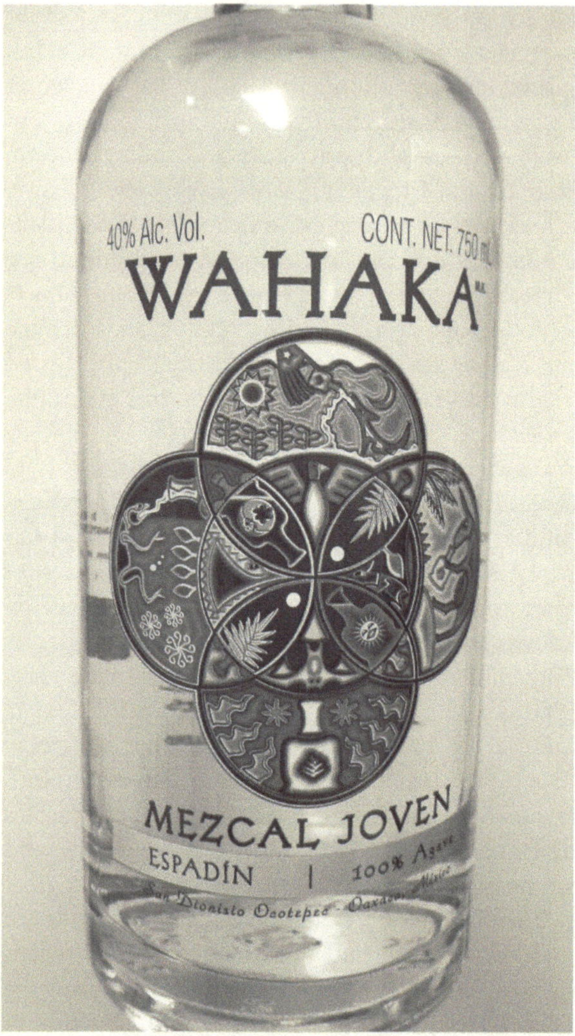

Figure 1.1 Wahaka brand mezcal features a logo reminiscent of an Indigenous Huichol yarn painting. Photo by author.

national and international recognition as the "spirit of Mexico" beginning in the nineteenth century. But as she herself hints, simply acknowledging tequila's success means failing to understand that it is embedded in the same colonial logic that also marginalized mezcal. Tequila, a type of mezcal, became popular at a time when Mexico was looking to escape its nonmodern image at home and abroad. A big part of its success story—in which it sets itself apart from mezcal, despite the physical similarities among all agave-distilled alcohols—involves overcoming historical stigmas associated with the consumption of "Native," non-European food and beverages. The Tequila region's historical, economic, and geographic conditions allowed the drink of the same name to align with a dominant narrative of Mexico as a modernizing, mestizo nation. The flip side of that coin is mezcal's historical devaluation as a drink associated with rural and Indigenous peoples in Mexico's southern backwaters, a historical trend that is now seeing a reversal. Ultimately, the present-day mezcal boom has emerged out of Mexico's colonial system and historically uneven development. The very factors that kept mezcal from being "discovered" and valued outside the region historically are creating new relations of power and inequality today.

Conquest and Coloniality

The marketing of mezcal today often relies on symbolism meant to evoke Oaxaca's Indigenous heritage, past and present. One stalwart commercial mezcal brand, Monte Alban, is literally named after one of the most famous pre-Hispanic archaeological sites in the state. Newer brands celebrate Indigeneity with arguably more sophisticated usages of Indigenous language (e.g., Zapotec place names like Geu Beez, or "River of Bees") and design, from bottles with stylized versions of pre-Hispanic animals to eye-catching versions of contemporary, Mexican Indigenous folk art. For example, the colorful logo for popular Wahaka brand mezcal is purposely reminiscent of a Huichol yarn painting, even though Huichol peoples hail from a geographically different part of Mexico (see figure 1.1). When I interviewed one of the brand owners, himself a Zapotec speaker from the community of San Dionisio Ocotepec in central Oaxaca, he endorsed the design because it symbolized Indigenous Mexico more generally to non-Indigenous consumers, his target audience. Meanwhile, visitors who stop at one of the many *palenques* (mezcal distilleries) on the highway leading east out of Oaxaca City might find visual representations linking mezcal to ancient Mexico, such as a painted mural featuring a pre-Hispanic figure in the act of cutting an agave, presumably for mezcal-making (see figure 1.2).

Marketing may evoke pre-Hispanic antiquity, but agave distillates are better understood as products of a historical process known as the Columbian Exchange. This term refers to the massive transfer of diseases, ideas, foods, and peoples between the New World and the Old World following Christopher Columbus's 1492 voyage, which forever altered food systems on both sides of the Atlantic (Nunn and Qian 2010).[3] Chiles, tomatoes, corn, and chocolate were just a few of the staple foodstuffs that traveled eastward, while the New World diet saw

Figure 1.2 A mural inside a Oaxacan distillery references ancient Mexico. Photo by author.

the introduction of livestock (cattle, pigs, sheep) and certain crops that would eventually become lucrative global commodities such as coffee and sugarcane (see Mintz 1985). The transfer of technology related to the production of food and drink was also a critical component of the Columbian Exchange; this included alcohol distillation, widely held to have been introduced into the Iberian Peninsula during the long period of Moorish occupation from 711 to 1492. Some have argued for the existence of pre-Hispanic distillation technology (Serra Puche and Lazcano Arce 2012). Archaeologists periodically find objects they believe support the claim of pre-Hispanic distillation, and one study even used replicas of pre-Hispanic vessels in an attempt to prove that distillation existed in parts of western Mexico as early as 3,500 years ago (McGovern et al. 2019). This claim is provocative and warrants further investigation. Nevertheless, the prevailing history of distillation in the Americas places its introduction after the Spanish invasion.

There is, however, ample evidence that fermented alcoholic intoxicants, brewed from a variety of fruits, grains, and other plants, were widespread in Mexico prior to the arrival of the Spanish (Bruman 2000).

A Mesoamerican tradition of fermented agave "beer" has been well documented in the archaeological and ethnological record, including in the Florentine, Magliabechiano, and Borbonicus codices. In these and other chronicles of the pre- and post-Conquest Aztec world, the deity Mayahuel presides over the agave plant, and by extension its frothy juice and the intoxicant, pulque, derived from it (Anders 1991; Boone 1983; Torrentera 2017). Known in Nahuatl as *octli*, this mildly alcoholic beverage (generally between 3 and 7 percent) made from the fermented juice or sap of the agave plant was produced extensively throughout the central highlands of Mexico as well as other regions of Mesoamerica (Parsons and Parsons 1990). Pulque was known by ancient Mexicans to be highly nutritious, and recent scientific analysis has shown it to be rich in vitamins, minerals, and probiotics (Escalante et al. 2016). It was also ritually significant. Pulque was served during religious festivals and celebrations such as weddings, fertility rites, and agricultural ceremonies. In the highly stratified world of the ancient Aztec, alcohol was considered a physically and symbolically potent substance that necessitated strict oversight. Access to pulque was therefore limited to elites, with the exception of the elderly and pregnant women among commoners, and public drunkenness was generally not tolerated (Anawalt 1993).

Pulque's revered status, not surprisingly, suffered during the Spanish invasion and subsequent rule, as did other foods and drinks associated with Mexican Indigenous populations, such as amaranth and maize (see Coe 1994). Mexico's colonial social order revolved around fine-grained yet malleable caste distinctions that were shaped not only by one's parentage, but also by taste and consumption habits. Spanish settlers replicated Old World foodstuffs and preparations to the extent possible, even though they invariably incorporated local culinary elements. Jeffrey M. Pilcher (1998) effectively illustrates how colonial social stratification was reinforced and communicated through the idiom of food. For example, drinking wine or cognac and eating *bolillos* (French rolls made from wheat)—and even the performative act of brushing breadcrumbs off one's jacket—functioned as markers of European civility. By the same token, consuming corn tortillas and agave-based drinks connoted an individual's low status. Within the colonial hierarchy, pulque therefore shifted away from the controlled, sacred realm to the everyday, popular culture of emerging Indigenous and mestizo underclasses. Elite disdain for pulque continued through the nineteenth century—though the ruling class was more than happy to collect taxes from it and other alcohol—even though the colonial-era caste system gave way to an emergent form of class-based social stratification toward the end of the eighteenth century (Chance 1978; Scardaville 1980).

As much as colonial elites strove to maintain a European lifestyle, efforts to replicate Old World food and drinks by importing or producing them locally were not always feasible, resulting in local substitutions with a healthy dose of improvisation. Many of today's iconic Mexican foods are, in fact, the result of culinary miscegenation over centuries, a synthesis of New and Old World ingredients and, importantly, technologies (Ayora-Diaz 2017). Pre-Hispanic steamed tamales took on a new flavor and texture with pork lard added to the masa, and more recently, the development of shaved, spit-roasted pork served in corn tortillas, the popular tacos al pastor, was a New World interpretation of the lamb shawarma brought to Mexico by Lebanese immigrants. And then there is the dish perhaps most exemplary of culinary *mestizaje*, the complex sauce known as mole poblano, first prepared in the colonial convents of Puebla; its long list of ingredients, including chiles, nuts, seeds, spices, fruits, and chocolate, among others, trace their origins to both sides of the Atlantic (Laudan and Pilcher 1999).

The introduction of hard alcohol was another significant transfer of technology and local adaptation that resulted from the Columbian Exchange. Having learned distillation technology during the Moorish occupation, the Spanish were by the time of the Conquest used to drinking both fermented and hard alcohol, a practice that accompanied their colonial enterprise. When their alcohol stores from Europe eventually ran low, they were faced with either importing more or making their own. Sugarcane and grapes were preferred source materials for distillation and, perhaps not surprisingly, two of the first crops introduced into the New World. However, the Spanish Crown enacted legislation aimed at protecting agricultural industries back in Spain from competition in the colonies, thereby limiting the growth of industries such as wine and brandy production in Mexico. At the same time that the Crown enacted protectionist measures, it also sought local sources of taxable revenue in the colonies. In the case of alcohol, this meant encouraging production from endemic materials not common to Iberia. By the end of the eighteenth century, the Spanish Crown was both taxing pulque and investing in the production of agave plants, whose cooked juice was distilled into the high-alcohol drink that came to be known as mezcal (De Barrios 2002). And while Mexico would eventually go on to develop its own homegrown alcohol industries based on traditions imported from Europe (e.g., beer, wine, brandy), pulque and the agave distillates that fall under the category of mezcal developed particular symbolic meanings throughout time, ones that mirrored the social and economic preoccupations of the developing Mexican nation.

Alcohol in Modernizing Mexico

"A Spanish visitor to Mexico City in the 1790s was impressed not only with its opulence, but also with the excessive numbers of drunks he saw throughout all sections of the metropolis" (Scardaville 1980, 645). Colonial historians have identified a strong relationship between alcohol consumption, crime, heresy, and rebellion (W. Taylor 1979). But just as important as these patterns in the colonial period were the new specialized drinking spaces that reinforced the social hierarchy, particularly in growing urban areas. Discussing alcohol abuse and tavern reform in colonial Mexico City, Michael C. Scardaville (1980, 644–645) writes that "alcoholic beverages (especially pulque, aguardiente, and tepache) and taverns (pulquerías, *casas de pulque, tepacherías,* and *vinaterías*) assumed a central role in the lives of the urban poor." And while Spanish and criollo elites undoubtedly counted among the ranks of the "excessive numbers of drunks" of the time, it was the consumers of traditional, homegrown alcohol, such as pulque, mezcal, and tepache, whose unchecked debauchery was viewed as the greater threat to societal stability.[4]

The Mexican elite's coexisting desire for and fear of modernization manifested in debates about drinking, and more specifically about drinking by the Indigenous and mestizo underclasses. These concerns did not fade after Mexico gained independence from Spain in 1821. If anything, they intensified as Mexico sought to shed its image as a colonial backwater and cultivate a modern, national identity. However, this was far from a simple matter. Like other newly independent Latin American nations, Mexico struggled with the question of how to define itself, and alcohol was frequently a point of conflict between liberal and conservative values. As Deborah Toner (2015) describes, these concerns primarily revolved around the spatial distribution of taverns, alcohol's potential subversion or reinforcement of gender norms linked to the ideology of liberal citizenship, and the transformation of lower-class, mixed-race, and Indigenous peoples into modern, patriotic subjects.

Arguments for and against drinking often expressed profound ambivalence toward alcohol vis-à-vis the national project of "Order and Progress," a motto adopted by various nineteenth-century Latin

American regimes. This includes the "progressive" dictatorship of Mexican president Porfirio Díaz, who ruled the country for thirty-one years between 1876 and 1911, a period known as the *porfiriato*. Díaz pursued an aggressive modernization plan predicated on direct foreign investment and new infrastructure, particularly to facilitate mining and petroleum exports. While Mexico's overall economy grew stronger during his presidency, vast segments of the population grew poorer, with the rural peasantry bearing much of the socioeconomic burden of development. As is often the case, alcohol was a salve for the disenfranchised, and popular drinking spaces such as cantinas and pulquerías were places of temporary escape for social groups that otherwise might direct their frustrations upward at those in power. At the same time, homegrown alcohol industries not only filled the void left by Spanish products since independence, they also showed potential for developing commercial products that could showcase Mexico's newest manufacturing capacities at home and abroad—a nascent consumer nationalism that cast specific products as unifying symbols of identity. This was the path of tequila, which I describe in greater detail below.

Running counter to these relatively favorable outlooks were ongoing concerns that alcohol only aggravated a predisposition for dangerous, destructive behavior among the Mexican poor, and particularly Indigenous populations. Toner (2015) highlights how racial and class distinctions contributed to these ideas, with pulque consumption becoming a locus of racial ideology (see also Ramírez Rodríguez 2018). At a time when Indigenous peoples were viewed as an impediment to the Porfirian regime's modernization agenda, the drink became a marker of "indigenous identity, along with sinfulness, barbarism, idolatry and other failings discursively associated with indigeneity" (Toner 2015, xxv). Toner also describes how the development of medical science in the 1890s and early 1900s further stigmatized alcohol consumption, but again, in a selective fashion that pathologized the drinking of only certain groups: Indigenous peoples, lower-class mestizos, Afro-descended individuals, and women across class and race. Yet in an ironic twist, alcoholism and its assumed provocation of mental illness, criminality, and physical degeneration were seen as consequences of modernity's uneven reach. In the end, regardless of whether alcohol and its abuses were the ill effects of or impediments to Mexico's modernizing agenda, the substance became a proxy for social exclusion and its justification.

Tequila and Mezcal in Mexico's Uneven Geography

> "It's mescal with me. . . . Tequila, no, that is healthful . . . and delightful. Just like beer. Good for you. But if I ever start to drink mescal again, I'm afraid, yes, that would be the end," the Consul said dreamily.
>
> Malcolm Lowry, *Under the Volcano* (1947)

In British writer Malcolm Lowry's 1947 novel *Under the Volcano*, protagonist Geoffrey Firmin, a former British consul, goes to Quauhnahuac (Cuernavaca), Mexico, where he continues a downward spiral of debilitating drinking that has already cost him his marriage and placed him on the fast track to an early death. The consul's excessive drinking manages to be both tragic and humorous, and mezcal's centrality to the narrative explains why *Under the Volcano* has found a new generation of readers among contemporary mezcal drinkers. But more than this, the novel and passages such as the one above are significant for portraying mezcal as an untamed, potentially dangerous spirit. In notable contrast to tequila—which eschews its popular reputation as a drink whose effects are wild and unpredictable, described here instead in tongue-in-cheek fashion as "healthful . . . and delightful. Just like beer"—mezcal signifies a potential end for even the most hardened alcoholic (Lowry 1947, 216). Lowry obviously employs this contrast to dramatic effect, but it also illustrates, rather ironically, the idea of tequila as a potentially more acceptable, even benign, source of debauchery than mezcal, which is accorded a sort of outlaw status throughout the book. The author's work, like that of other artists, was a product of its time, raising the question of what conditions led to these distinct portrayals of tequila and mezcal in the first place.

To contextualize Lowry's prose, we must consider that the twentieth and twenty-first centuries witnessed a massive shift in attitudes among the elite (as well as those of a burgeoning middle class) toward alcohol, and particularly locally produced intoxicants. During the Mexican Revolution (1910–1920) and the nationalist period it catalyzed, there were still deep concerns about lower-class debauchery, including the barrier alcohol represented to Indigenous assimilation to mestizo society. This, however, did not impede the commercialization and valorization of tequila as a national industry, a process that was underway at the time but not fully realized until the twentieth century. In fact, tequila's commercial rise was no historical accident; its path helps clarify why mezcal was such a latecomer to the global spirits market.

Mexico's physical and cultural geography was especially critical to the drinks' divergent paths. As Oscar J. Martínez (2016) persuasively argues, the country's uneven terrain, industry, and population distribution resulted in the concentration of economic and social capital in certain regions of the country, while other parts—particularly in the south—remained on the economic periphery. Within this geography, tequila was much better positioned than mezcal for commercialization, for several reasons. First, the original tequila-producing area was located exclusively within the western state of Jalisco, around the town of Tequila and in the region known as Los Altos, both within relative proximity (65 kilometers and 135 kilometers, respectively) of the state capital, Guadalajara (see map 1.2).[5] The economically bustling city (presently the third largest in Mexico) has long facilitated interest and capital investment in the adjacent, tequila-producing regions. The area has historically benefited from transportation networks. Railroads connected it to northern Mexico and the US border, as well as to the political hub of Mexico City; it was also in proximity to the port of San Blas, which became the primary Pacific port when Acapulco (in the state of Guerrero) was shut down during Mexico's War of Independence. Second, agriculture and related industries have traditionally been enmeshed in the system of landed, revenue-generating estates known as haciendas, which developed in the seventeenth and eighteenth centuries out of the Spanish encomienda system found throughout Latin America (Knight 1991). Unlike small-scale subsistence farming, with its emphasis on household production and consumption, haciendas tended toward agricultural production for regional and national markets and relied on a low-wage labor force drawn from a subdued peasantry that had managed to survive the genocide of Indigenous peoples in what was once known as Nueva Galicia (Ginzberg 2020).[6] The orientation to external markets favored single commodity crops such as rice, wheat, sugarcane, tobacco, and, importantly, agave, which in time became overwhelmingly represented by one domesticated variety, *agave tequilana*, popularly known as blue agave. Moreover, the hacienda system placed control over local labor and land rights into the hands of a few, a consolidation of power that only intensified during the *porfiriato*. The consolidation of power would ultimately sow seeds of discontent, leading to the Revolution. But in the preceding period, haciendas expanded their market reach, benefiting from the modern transportation and banking infrastructure created during Díaz's liberal dictatorship (Gaytán 2014). Tequila, then, was well poised for commercialization, including the branding that would elevate tequila's status and the creation of market channels both within Mexico and to the United States and Europe. In synergistic fashion, the commercialization and formal regulation of tequila resulted in enormous tax revenue, much of which was funneled back into Jalisco's growing regional economy.

José Orozco (2014) chronicles the rise of the Sauza family in Jalisco. Family patriarch Cenobio Sauza, in the early 1870s, became the first maker to export the mezcal that came to be recognized by the geographic indicator "tequila" to the United States and Europe. The tequila entrepreneur obviously hoped to expand his market, but this was not only a bid to gain international buyers. At a time when the Mexican upper crust still distinguished itself from the masses by adopting foreign tastes in everything from music to fashion, Sauza rightly intuited that his compatriots would be more likely to drink tequila if it had European and American consumers' stamp of approval—a colonialist mentality that equated foreignness with superiority. With this in mind, he entered his tequila into the 1893 World's Columbian Exposition in Chicago to show the world that it was "simultaneously an authentic product of Mexico and a clean, non-disgust-inducing, civilized, and cosmopolitan liquor like cognac, champagne, or brandy" (Orozco 2014, 191). Today, while Sauza may not represent the high end of the tequila market, it ranks among the most recognized liquor brands in the world and is virtually everywhere recognized as a "Mexican" product, despite being owned by a multinational liquor company headquartered in Chicago (Martineau 2015a).[7] Tequila continued to gain in popularity throughout the late nineteenth century and into the twentieth, as other Jalisco-based family brands established themselves as long-term players in the market. Notable among them was José Cuervo, one of Sauza's main competitors, who launched a company that today supplies nearly one-fifth of the tequila sold worldwide.

If the *porfiriato* laid the economic and infrastructural conditions for tequila's ascendance, then the Mexican Revolution and the postrevolutionary nationalism it engendered sealed the deal by winning consumer hearts and minds. In a move to unify the country's geographically and culturally disparate populations, the Mexican government undertook one of the most aggressive programs of cultural nationalism in the western hemisphere (Joseph, Rubenstein, and Zolov 2001). Popular culture provided abundant source material for a collective identity, referred to in Spanish as *mexicanidad* (Mexicanness). Indeed, some of Mexico's most enduring symbols were created and promoted during this period, including public monuments, mural art, and folkloric dance (Alonso

2008; Nájera Ramírez 1989). Nonindustrial craft work (*artesanía*) associated with Indigenous peoples and campesinos, too, became a source of national pride, as well as a target of state-led rural developmental programs (López 2010; Novelo 1976). A tourism industry incorporating these unique Mexican cultural sites, arts, and performances emerged in the late 1920s (Berger 2006). US tourists were one obvious market. Yet this was also a time when the Mexican upper class and nascent middle class started to identify with and consume cultural products as part of a collective national "Mexican" patrimony. As Eugenio Mercado López (2022, 41) succinctly puts it, "the 1910 Mexican Revolution allowed citizens to discover their country."

The selective valorization of popular culture included cantina culture and, with it, tequila. In the postrevolutionary imaginary, the cantina became the romanticized backdrop for a certain male archetype—valiant, tequila-swilling, and ready to fight—embodied by revolutionary folk hero Francisco "Pancho" Villa. In real life Villa was a teetotaler who, inspired by the temperance movement in the United States, advocated for a prohibition on alcohol in Mexico, going so far as to outlaw drinking when he was the governor of the northern border state of Chihuahua (Gaytán 2014). But that did not prevent cantinas, tequila, and a particular masculine ideal from becoming intrinsically linked in Mexican popular culture. Tequila was potent, but in a socially acceptable way. Marketing campaigns played a direct role in this. One tequila was quite literally named "Pancho Villa" when it launched in the 1960s. And, according to *The New American Bartender's Guide*, the original way to order a tequila was "Pancho Villa style," immediately recognizable today as a shot of tequila served with a lime wedge and salt (Poister 1999).

A successful national film and music industry also spread Mexican popular culture to a consumer base throughout Latin America and beyond. The golden age of Mexican cinema, the period from 1936 to 1956, brought scenes of agave-filled landscapes and protagonists drowning their sorrows over a bottle of tequila to audiences in Cuba, Colombia, and elsewhere, even as far away as Yugoslavia (Irwin and Castro Ricalde 2013). Popular music genres that frequently celebrated drinking and Mexican cantina culture, such as *rancheras* (ranch music), mariachi, and corridos, had a similarly wide reach in the Spanish-speaking world and beyond.[8] This is one reason that a selective set of cultural symbols from the state of Jalisco became conflated with the idea of Mexicanness itself: not only tequila and mariachi, but also *charreadas* (Mexican rodeos) and the *jarabe tapatío*, or a dance performance by *tapatíos* (people from Guadalajara and the Jalisco Highlands). Tellingly, the English translation of *jarabe tapatío* as the "Mexican hat dance" replaced its regional reference with a more generic, national one, with Jalisco becoming interchangeable with Mexico itself. It also did not hurt that *tapatíos* were known for their "traditional" values and fair-skinned good looks, including green or blue eyes and red hair, considered indicative of European bloodlines (P. Taylor 1933).

Oaxaca, in contrast, occupied a very different position in both the physical and social geography of Mexico. Spanish colonialism distinctly organized the society and economy of Oaxaca so that it did not feed the nationalist myth in the same way that Jalisco did, and the perception of agave spirits reflects this. In contrast to tequila's rise to prominence as a national symbol, Oaxacan mezcal languished as a mostly regional drink, shedding its low-quality reputation only toward the end of the twentieth century. In the way that tequila's trajectory was not purely happenstance, mezcal's, too, was shaped by geography and socioeconomic conditions. Located in a mountainous region in the far south of the country, Oaxaca was for much of its history excluded from the large-scale agricultural and industrial development characteristic of central and northern Mexico. Unlike other regions, Oaxaca never developed large-scale mining operations or an extensive hacienda system. To this day, Oaxaca is also one of the poorest places in the country, a fact obscured by the veneer of prosperity lent by its boutique tourism industry.

If rugged topography made transportation and communication difficult, it also meant that Oaxaca historically maintained a high degree of ethnolinguistic diversity in comparison with other parts of Mexico. Colonial Oaxaca was also overwhelmingly Indigenous; as late as the 1790s, an estimated 90 percent of the population was counted as "Indian" (Chance and Taylor 1977, 457). More importantly, this large Native population, in contrast with Jalisco's peasantry, maintained relative economic independence and control over large areas of land, with subsistence farming taking precedence over commodity crop production (W. Taylor 1972). Whereas the hacienda system flourished in much of the country, Oaxacan Indigenous communities maintained control over much of the local land and natural resources. They also regulated significant sectors of the internal market, which comprised an extensive, interregional system that circulated goods (including locally produced mezcal and pulque) within and between communities (S. Cook and Diskin 1975). With regard to externally oriented production, from the sixteenth to the nineteenth centuries, Oaxaca was one of the world's main suppliers of cochineal, a valuable red dye sourced from a cactus-dwelling insect (Baskes 2000). As Carlos Marichal Salinas (2018, 256–257) notes, the "considerable population density of peasant communities in the mountainous territory of Oaxaca was an important precondition for the highly labour-intensive cultivation of the nopal plants on which the cochineal insect thrived." But this economic boom did not last. The invention of synthetic dye in the mid-nineteenth century greatly diminished global demand for cochineal and, with it, the wealth it generated.

Oaxaca's economic import began to decline, and by the time Mexico gained its independence in 1821 it was already something of a colonial backwater. Porfirian-era plans for building infrastructure and courting foreign capital did not unfold there as they did in Jalisco and other parts of Mexico. Once again, geography and demographics were critical. Oaxaca's main urban center was the small capital of the same name, which sat landlocked in the center of the state at a confluence of several imposing mountain ranges. There, a small, oligarchic class, self-conscious of its European roots and status, concentrated its commercial and social activity, sometimes in physical proximity to the diverse Indigenous communities that surrounded it—but always culturally worlds apart from these communities. In turn, Indigenous peoples' relative political and economic autonomy was a disincentive to national and foreign investors alike: Native communities that did not readily embrace the idea of private property were seen as an impediment to the type of capitalist penetration characteristic of Porfirian Mexico. Consequently, conditions for large-scale trade and commerce did not materialize. This meant that most rural industries never developed beyond regional or local markets (S. Cook 2014). This was true as well for locally produced mezcal and pulque; the large landed estates and commerce networks that provided favorable conditions for the rise of commercial tequila enterprises like those of the Sauza and Cuervo families simply did not have an analog in Oaxaca. Mezcal mostly remained in the countryside and in working-class drinking establishments in urban areas that were supplied by small-scale, rural producers.

Historian William B. Taylor (1972) characterized the Mexican Revolution as a struggle for land and economic independence rather than political inclusion. As such, the Revolution's rallying cry of "Tierra y libertad" (Land and Liberty) did not reverberate in Oaxaca as it did in other parts of Mexico. Rural communities simply had not been dispossessed from their land and deprived of their basic livelihoods as had subsistence farmers in other parts of the country. But even though

Oaxaca did not figure predominantly in the revolutionary campaign, its large Indigenous population drew the attention of the postrevolutionary government, whose political ideology of *indigenismo* promoted a close relationship between Indigenous groups and the modern Mexican state (Knight 1990). *Indigenismo* targeted two forms of Indigenous materiality for state-led development: handicrafts and pre-Hispanic archaeological monuments (Errington 1998; López 2010). Oaxaca had both in abundance, which aligned it with the postrevolutionary ideology of craft as made by Indigenous groups. Scholars have argued that nationalist cultural projects ultimately proved more symbolic than effective in producing true social and material gains for Indigenous communities in Oaxaca and elsewhere (Vaughan and Lewis 2006); indeed, racism not only continued but was itself often propagated through *indigenista* programs. But what *indigenismo* did do is create an environment in which early twentieth-century artists, intellectuals, and writers aestheticized and commodified Mexican Indigeneity through their work. Part of a modernist artistic movement, Frida Kahlo, D. H. Lawrence, Edward Weston, Elsie Clews Parsons, and others found an exotic charm in Oaxaca's persistent poverty, which they expressed in their creative works, whether novels, photographs, paintings, or ethnographic writings.

Indigenismo and those for whom Oaxaca served as a backdrop for modernist nostalgia unwittingly laid the foundation for what the region would become at the end of the twentieth century and into the twenty-first: a globally recognized arts and culture destination largely untransformed by the trappings of widespread industrialization and rural-urban integration found throughout other parts of Mexico. If we understand mezcal as reflecting the historical characteristics of the place in which it proliferated, it becomes clear as to why the drink is only now having its so-called moment. It is no coincidence that some of the earliest artisanal mezcals to arrive in the US market in the 1990s were brought by American artists who "discovered" them as part of their creative journeys (see Cooper and Martineau 2018). Mezcal is metaphor and proxy for Oaxaca as place—that is, how people treat mezcal is how people treat Oaxaca. In the context of global consumerism, Oaxaca has become shorthand for that which is authentic, Indigenous, and culturally enduring; and mezcal, once the derided drink of Mexico's Indigenous backwater is now celebrated, and curated, rather than stigmatized.

We are undoubtedly living in an era in which descriptors such as "craft," "maker," and "artisanal" have taken on cultural and economic currency to the point of cliché and certainly comedic parody. In the 1990s, few would have taken Oaxacan craft to include locally produced mezcal, as "craft" implied material forms like rugs, pottery, and wood carving, rarely food or drink. In the next chapter, I discuss how a new, historically conditioned craft imaginary has evolved and expanded to encompass Oaxacan mezcal. While mezcal may demonstrate qualities that lead to its categorization as craft in today's marketplace, such distinctions ultimately rest on the person who is doing the selling as much as, if not more than, the product itself.

2 | Mezcal in the New Craft Imaginary

> With tequila, the pinas [hearts] are cooked in large industrial ovens, known as autoclaves, which are large, stainless-steel industrial pressure cookers. (note: there are other methods of cooking and crushing the pinas but this is the most common). Then the cooked agave is shredded and fermented blah blah blah. So uninteresting. So industrial. So mass production. So boring! (Can you feel the mezcal bias brewing?)
>
> —John P. McEvoy, "Tequila vs. Mezcal" (2018)

It was the summer of 2013, and Carlos and I were seated in a small, roadside café in Santiago Matatlán, an Indigenous Zapotec-speaking town of roughly 3,400 inhabitants and the self-proclaimed "mezcal capital of the world," forty-eight kilometers east of the capital city of Oaxaca. We had met earlier that morning, when a friend asked me to accompany him and his boss from the Oaxacan Secretariat of Tourism and Economic Development as they escorted Carlos to meet some of Matatlán's mezcal producers. He had flown in from Guadalajara just the day before, on a mission to find a mezcal to add to his product line of tequilas. It was notable that these government officials were willing to spend their Sunday privately chauffeuring him around.

"Well, you know, I do make Justin Timberlake's tequila. And my products are in Walmarts all over the world," Carlos said. His words were obviously meant to impress, what with their connotations of celebrity and worldwide commercial distribution. However, he neglected to consider that they might, in fact, have the opposite effect, linking the alcoholic spirit to a US-based big-box store viewed by some as the epitome of unbridled consumerism and mass production—the antithesis of the narrative driving the mezcal boom.

As referenced by his comment, he was a joint owner of a successful Jalisco-based company, Destilería Santa Lucía, which produced a number of tequila brands. Among them was the brand 901, owned by Justin Timberlake of US boy band NSYNC fame and reportedly named for his childhood area code in Memphis, Tennessee. (In 2014, the 901 brand was acquired by Jalisco-based Sauza, the second-largest tequila brand in the world after José Cuervo.)

We had visited five different *palenques* (mezcal distilleries) over the course of the morning, and I had watched as Carlos's frustration had visibly grown. At the last facility we visited, he wandered around aimless and bored, leaving my companions and me to talk to the producer and his wife, who had interrupted their midday meal to attend to us by patiently doling out samples of each of their products.

Later, as we sat waiting for our food to arrive, Carlos expressed his disappointment with the mezcals he had sampled. In his words they "were nothing special." But the biggest source of his disillusion came from the fact that no one was willing to immediately sell him the quantity of mezcal he wanted at the price he was offering: twenty thousand liters at forty pesos per liter (at the time, just under three US dollars). The lowest price that any producer had quoted him was seventy pesos per liter, and I had assured him that this was on the low end of the going price. I added that trying to purchase such a large quantity of artisanal mezcal on demand was nearly impossible, as only the largest commercial distilleries in Oaxaca would be likely to have that volume available. There was, in fact, no solution to his problem. Not only was he making demands that could not be met by a still largely nonindustrial system of production, but he had not anticipated that Matatlán producers were aware of the increasing market value of their craft mezcal. In the not-so-distant past, some producers might have, out of desperation, sold their product at a loss, accepting a price even below their material and labor costs. But times had changed—at least in Matatlán. Indeed, at the last *palenque* we had visited, his attempt to lowball the producer had been met with polite defiance. He may have been unwilling or unable to grasp the differences in scale and production methods between the tequila he sold and Oaxacan mezcal, but they were certainly not lost on the producer.

"Pero señor, hay que reconocer que es un producto 100% artesanal" (But sir, you need to recognize that this is a 100 percent artisanal product).

Eventually resigned to fact that he was not going to secure a mezcal deal on that trip, Carlos commanded that we return to the city so he could prepare for his departure from Oaxaca the following day. Scenes like this repeat daily as an influx of would-be buyers scout out potential producers to add to or launch their mezcal line. However, what stood out to me in this case was the producer's appeal to the artisanal nature of his product. He held firm on his price because he knew the *value of craft in the current market*—something that would have been much less likely in previous eras, when mezcal producers would have been happy just to move their product, sometimes even taking a loss.

Figure 2.1 An artisan still maker with his handmade copper pots. Photo by author.

At the heart of this chapter is the question of why mezcal was able to transcend its seemingly humble origins to become one of Mexico's most sought-after products. Part of the answer lies in the epigraph from John McEvoy, a self-styled mezcal expert and author of *Holy Smoke! It's Mezcal! A Complete Guide from Agave to Zapotec* (2014) as well as the popular blog *Mezcal PhD*. While tequila may still be the quintessential Mexican drink, McEvoy, like many mezcal evangelists, is turned off by the arguably blasé nature of tequila, which he attributes to its overt commercialization and industrial mode of production. According to this logic, the fact that tequila is no longer a primarily artisanal or craft product makes it inherently less desirable than its so-called smoky cousin, mezcal. But if mezcal is allegedly so much more "interesting" than tequila, why did it take so long for mezcal to gain traction in the marketplace, its boom taking place as recently as 2010?

At first glance, mezcal's popularity may appear to be a by-product of the tequila industry's expansive reach. They are, after all, both agave spirits, and as we saw in the previous chapter, tequila has enjoyed commercial success in Mexico and abroad for years. It is not uncommon for aficionados to discover mezcal after first becoming tequila connoisseurs. Yet finding one's way from tequila to mezcal is not an inevitable progression; nor does it signal the development of more educated or refined tastes, as McEvoy insinuates. Indeed, some of the most die-hard mezcal fans I know, particularly those under the age of fifty, show little interest in or prior experience with tequila. If anything, their tastes in alcoholic libations lean more toward other craft spirits, cocktails, beer, and natural wines. Therefore, such late-to-the-party stories of mezcal's popularity do not fully explain the wider conditions that allowed it to flourish.

Not only did mezcal have its moment in the first decades of the twenty-first century, but that moment was also part of a wider global resurgence of interest in craft as both object and process. The idea of craftwork is obviously not new. However, today's new craft imaginary, which arose in the early 2000s during a time of socioeconomic crisis, created an urgency to know the story of the objects we consume—and what a story there was to be told about mezcal! It was one that aligned perfectly with a desire for human connection and a return to the handmade (see figure 2.1). Some would argue that Mexican federal regulation legitimized the spirit, but this chapter shows how a new craft imaginary created the broader context for mezcal's story—and market—to fully unfold.

Craft Imaginaries

Because of craft's association with the handmade, we often assume that it has existed from time immemorial—and that is not entirely wrong. Indeed, the forms of skilled knowledge and practice we define as craft are often considered among the qualities that make us uniquely human. Nevertheless, the word *craft*, and, by extension, our awareness of it as a sphere of production distinct from the mechanical, is relatively recent. Craft, as the term is generally used today, is a product of the Industrial Revolution and the broader philosophical and artistic movement of modernism that it gave rise to. Craft was invented as industry's "other," a counterpart to the ideas of progress and upheaval whose function was to hold space for the human maker in a machine-driven age (Adamson 2013). It served as an "antidote to what Max Weber described as the progressive disenchantment of the world, the replacement of a pre-modern social order, with its mythical orientation to the world, by a bureaucratized, secular modernity" (Brulotte and Montoya 2019, 17).[1]

Yet while we may agree that craft contains an appeal to the handmade, we must also recognize that the term and related concepts of authenticity, heritage, and tradition do not have a fixed meaning or referent. Elsewhere, M. J. R. Montoya and I suggest that analyzing craft in today's global economy "entails moving beyond craft as a specific category of object or practice in order to understand it as a concept emerging out of specific socioeconomic relationships" (Brulotte and Montoya 2019, 17). Central to defining craft, then, is identifying how ideas about past modes of production are mobilized in specific moments and to specific ends within the modern capitalist system.

Moreover, we can observe a historical pattern in which craft takes on heightened significance during times of economic and social crisis. Emma Bell, M. Tina Dacin, and Maria Laura Toraldo (2021, 13) note that during such periods, craft imaginaries often stand "as an alternative to the perceived failure of industrial production and consumption to deliver societal benefits that have been promised." The authors draw on philosopher Charles Taylor's (2003, 6) concept of modern social imaginaries, defined as the "way our [Western] contemporaries imagine the societies they inhabit and sustain." More than just a set of ideas, social imaginaries are an entire repertory of understandings and practices through which a group of people work toward a collective moral purpose and moral order. For Bell, Dacin, and Toraldo (2021, 4), craft is a particular type of social imaginary, one organized around the ideals of nonmechanized, nonalienated human labor. And though craft may take on a backward-looking or nostalgic hue, they argue that the "historical persistence of the craft imaginary reflects its value as a collective construction which has legitimating potential in challenging dominant social imaginaries and providing alternatives." Thus, appealing to past modes of production like the handmade may serve a future-oriented purpose, allowing humans to reenvision the construction of their material and social worlds.

If the industrial age of the late nineteenth and early twentieth centuries gave rise to the modern craft imaginary, two other historical moments saw its resurgence. The first coincided with the countercultural movement (colloquially known as "hippie culture") that began in the United States in the 1960s and continued into the 1970s, spreading throughout much of the Western world. Historian David Farber (2016, 409–410) cites the centrality of craft for countercultural practitioners who, to the extent possible, "wanted handmade lives" and "were dedicated to building communities focused on human-scale production that valued artisanal competency and community utility." This value manifested in everything from the clothes they wore to the foods they cultivated and prepared to the homes they built. Some sought to completely escape the capitalist economic system. Yet, Farber notes, "most made a kind of separate peace with both capitalism and the pleasures of material comfort and consumption" (411). Thus, even those on the fringes of the economic mainstream could not wholly escape it and, in many cases, created new markets for goods and services aligned with their values. The upscale Whole Foods grocery chain, frequently derided as "Whole Paycheck," is a good example of this; it started in 1978 as a small natural foods store called SaferWay in Austin, Texas.

The most recent craft imaginary emerged in the wake of the 2008 financial crisis. Disillusioned by a global market driven by corporations and economies of scale, consumers shifted their attention to forms of production they perceived to be more socially, economically, and environmentally sustainable (Bell, Dacin, and Toraldo 2021, 4). This period saw an acceleration of the contemporary DIY movement, craftivism (activism focused on craft practices), and artisanal culture broadly defined. It also witnessed a push to "reframe craft from a form of hobby-work to a viable form of commerce" (Suddaby, Ganzin, and Minkus 2017, 6). Not surprisingly, the marketplace evolved to accommodate new forms of do-what-you-love entrepreneurship, such as home brewers turning their skills to opening craft breweries. At the same time, digital technologies enabled a new generation of direct-to-consumer businesses that bypassed brick-and-mortar stores and other wholesalers altogether, including hobby crafters who set up "shops" for their wares on Etsy, a platform that had launched in 2005, just a few years before the financial crisis. By late 2009 it was announced that Etsy had started turning a profit, and by late 2011 the company had more than ten million members, with a reported eight hundred thousand active shops (Eldridge 2024).

At the global level, reviving and creating new artisan supply chains is more than a passing fad; it has become a lucrative business model. A 2020 article in *Entrepreneur* magazine, "Why Artisans Will Be Powerful in the New Economy," observed that "when the 2008 global financial crisis drove markets down by nearly a quarter, demand for artisan products kept growing—doubling in value from just six years before. In 2017, the global handicrafts market reached a value of $526.5 billion and is set to almost double in growth again over the next three years" (Polites 2020). The very fact that craft goods are now considered a legitimate sector that warrants measure points to their rising importance among the cultural and creative industries.

In the new craft imaginary, the world is conceived as one enormous, artisanal marketplace, providing everything from handcrafted Turkish slippers (Sabah) to small-batch, chef-endorsed Vietnamese fish sauce (Son) to a range of tastefully minimalist, handmade goods for the home (New York–based lifestyle brand the Citizenry)—this last including woven pillowcases and "Mercado Storage Baskets" from Oaxaca and Guerrero, Mexico, respectively. These are all examples of the "enrichment economy" theorized by Luc Boltanski and Arnaud Esquerre (2020). Enrichment is the process by which goods and services moving through a global value chain "command a higher market price without any visible change in material inputs to their production or the amount of time spent in producing and consuming them" (Vogel and Shipman 2023). Not only has the global handmade become widely available, but the enrichment economy has rebranded as premium or luxury goods some everyday items (shoes, fish sauce, baskets), including some that in a different time or place may have been associated with low status or poverty. For instance, the inexpensive leather huaraches (sandals) found in markets throughout Mexico may now be purchased online from a company called Espiritu, which offers "huarache shoes made for the 21st century," with a "classic" women's pair going for US$125 (Espiritu, n.d.).

In light of the above, then, it is no coincidence that mezcal's popularity soared when it did. Mezcal had all the qualities to become a craft spirit—handmade by rural and Indigenous producers in a remote corner of Mexico—it just needed someone (the right person) to tell the right story.

When Mezcal Became "Craft"

"To be perceived as premium and artisanal," writes Maureen Ballatori (2022) in *Forbes* magazine, "brands must understand who they are speaking to, know the story they are telling, provide an attractive physical presence and navigate the mediums of engagement." The contemporary mezcal market demonstrates all these elements, a reminder that business principles are now equally embedded in product value chains with the raw ingredients that make up the products themselves. From this perspective, mezcal is as dependent on the quality of the agave plant or production process as it is on the strategic factors that give mezcal a competitive advantage in the marketplace.

Domingo García Garza (2022) argues that "traditional mezcal" is an invention of the modern market, as are, I would add, most other classifications and descriptors currently applied to the drink. Furthermore, the insistence on mezcal's authenticity—whether coded as traditional, craft, or artisanal—is more often commentary on those who are selling and consuming it than on the mezcal itself, including its quality. As an aside, it is generally presumed that "craft" mezcal is a superior product because it is arguably made with better materials, demonstrates more care for the process, and is produced in smaller quantities. This is familiar logic, one applied to a variety of artisanal food and drink—think of a handmade, cave-aged cheddar cheese versus a block of grocery store Kraft brand cheddar—and one that frequently shapes comparisons between mezcal and tequila. Yet as I show in the next chapter, learning to appreciate a craft mezcal is not simply a matter of individual taste, and when presented with a range of mezcal options, the average person may be just as likely to enjoy an "industrially" produced mezcal as an artisanal one. To wit: a friend in Oaxaca recounted the story of a blind tasting he attended in which participants sampled a variety of mezcals, ranging from small-batch artisanal to more commercial products; everyone was shocked when the overwhelming favorite turned out to be a bottle of Zignum, a mezcal brand made at one of the largest industrial facilities in Oaxaca.[2] What is telling in this anecdote is not that Zignum came out on top in the taste test, but that the tasters themselves seemed so shocked by the outcome.

To understand how we got to this point, we must briefly go back to the now widely circulated story of mezcal's "discovery" in the early 1990s by American artist Ron Cooper. Like so many artists before him, Cooper traveled throughout Oaxaca looking for artistic inspiration, which led him to try an "amazing elixir" that was then relatively unknown outside of Mexico (Cooper and Martineau 2018). Cooper enthusiastically loaded his truck with his find, but on his way back home to Taos, New Mexico, he was stopped at the border, where his cargo was confiscated by US customs. This was a setback, but only a minor one, and it made the artist more determined than ever to share his discovery with others. The Mexican federal government's establishment of a denomination of origin (DO) for mezcal in 1994 set the stage for Cooper to fully enter the market with his brand Del Maguey Mezcal, founded the following year. He eventually set up headquarters in Teotitlán del Valle, a Zapotec-speaking village about thirty kilometers from Oaxaca City known for its hand-dyed woolen rugs and the restaurant Tlamanalli, featuring cuisine by the now-famous Indigenous chef Abigail Mendoza Ruiz.

Marie Sarita Gaytán (2019, 5) insightfully analyzes Cooper's rise to become the "godfather" of craft mezcal, including his winning the

Figure 2.2 Mezcal producer Faustino García Vásquez poses with an original bottle of Del Maguey Chichicapa. The label features a picture of him holding a tube made from *carrizo* (reed) that is used to siphon mezcal and measure its alcohol content. Photo by author.

award for best-tasting mezcal in the 1999 World Spirits Championships (albeit a severely limited playing field) and the James Beard Award for Outstanding Wine, Beer, or Spirits Professional in 2017. She attributes his success to the ability to cultivate what she calls "artisan kinship" and "craft celebrity" within the Del Maguey brand. She describes artisan kinship as "a fictive sensibility that strengthens producer-consumer relations as it allays a range of marketplace manifestations, including 'the anomie and placeness produced by globalization.'" The idiom of family belonging—within a Del Maguey family headed by the celebrity persona of Cooper himself, that is—proved a powerful mechanism for creating brand loyalty. For his part, Cooper appeared both accessible and omnipotent, "granting interviews, giving talks, meeting customers, communicating with consumers via his website, being responsive to social media inquiries, [and] traveling to spirits' conventions" (Gaytán 2019, 5). Indeed, Del Maguey was a textbook example of the elements that Ballatori (2022) identifies as key to marketing a premium and artisanal brand. Cooper's adventure narrative and personal engagement strongly resonated with consumers, as did Del Maguey's focus on supporting small craft producers and farmers. In keeping with this focus, some of the company's earliest packaging involved clear glass bottles featuring a picture of the producer (see figure 2.2). It later redesigned its packaging, employing instead a distinctive green glass (Cooper once remarked to me that one of his goals was "to see a line of green [Del Maguey] bottles behind every bar"). Sporting labels with the brand's trademarked slogan "Single Village Mezcal" and stylized, colorful artwork by sculptor Kenneth Price, an old friend of Cooper's, the new packaging included a palm basket handwoven by Indigenous Zapotec women. Importantly, Del Maguey's development coincided with and helped fuel the craft cocktail renaissance, as Cooper and his team embarked on an aggressive educational program to introduce bar and restaurant professionals around the United States to his product. This also included leading personalized tours to Oaxacan villages to meet his producers.

The artisan kinship and craft celebrity Del Maguey cultivated proved enduring. In 2017 Cooper announced that he was selling his majority share in Del Maguey to Pernod Ricard, the world's second-largest liquor conglomerate. The buyout reflected a trend of large corporations acquiring artisanal food and beverage brands, such as Unilever's purchase of Ben & Jerry's ice cream and the Kraft Heinz Company's purchase of Green & Black's, known for its organic, ethically sourced chocolate. Notably, not all such acquisitions or relationships are able to avoid consumer disillusionment, such as when it was revealed in 2012 that artisan tea bag company Teapigs was owned by the same international Indian conglomerate that owns Tetley. Yet Del Maguey was so firmly cemented in the craft imaginary that, as Gaytán notes (2019, 1), "there was little fan backlash" as a result of the buyout.

Ron Cooper and Del Maguey may be credited as the first purveyors of craft mezcal in the United States, but others soon followed. In 2007 Jonathan Barbieri, an American painter and self-described "distiller" living in Oaxaca, launched his Pierde Almas mezcal, the name based on a series of paintings and drawings that, according to his website, "conjure the world of the cantinas he frequented during the 1980s and 90s in Oaxaca, Mexico" (Barbieri, n.d.). Oaxaca-based painter Willy Olguín launched his Los Amantes brand in 2003, and in 2004 American expat John Rexer began bringing mezcal from Oaxaca farther south to Antigua, Guatemala, to sell at his popular bar Café No Sé, resulting in the founding of his brand Ilegal in 2006. Mezcal Vago (*vago* translating to vagabond) started when a young American surfer named Judah Kuper found mezcal, along with a woman's love, on the Oaxacan coast, building his brand around the mezcal produced by his new father-in-law, Aquilino García López, in the village of Candelaria Yegolé (see Mezcal Vago, n.d.). As with Del Maguey, all these craft mezcals feature narratives of discovery, clandestine operations, or artistic projects as central to their brands, stories that may forge a sense of personal connection with consumers, even if only imagined.

In hindsight, it is easy to see how the mezcal that Cooper and others brought to market was primed for inclusion in the new craft imaginary. It was handmade in small batches by people and not machines, qualities that the tequila industry had largely abandoned over the years as it became, for the most part, a multinational corporate enterprise (Martineau 2015a). Further, most craft mezcal came from Oaxaca, a region of Mexico that was at this time developing into a global epicenter of gastronomy and art. Positioning mezcal as a manifestation of both proved to be a brilliant marketing strategy. Yet while mezcal's craft status seems to have been a foregone conclusion, its nuances were defined over a period of time in which people anxiously negotiated authenticity, the product all the while responding to changing market conditions.

Artisanal Unease

"When they're using the term *ancestral* [in the new rules], they have very little idea what it means, in my opinion," said Steve Olson, an internationally recognized wine and spirits expert who provided business consulting and educational services through his New York–based company Aka Wine Geek. Olson was more than just a concerned citizen; he was deeply invested in mezcal's commercial success. He first met Ron Cooper at the Grand Central margarita competition in 1995, and almost from the beginning became indispensable to extending the brand's reach, hosting Del Maguey tastings and fostering collaborations with otherwise inaccessible food and drink industry insiders (Gaytán 2019, 5).

Olson made this comment to Cooper and me over lunch in the spring of 2015. He was referencing a highly contentious proposal to modify the existing Norma Oficial Mexicana NOM-070-SCFI-1994, the Mexican federal guidelines for mezcal's DO, in place since 1994. These guidelines stipulated that all commercially sold mezcal be labeled according to three new categories: industrial, artisanal, and ancestral. While all types of mezcal are required to be made from 100 percent agave, each category contained its own criteria for permissible types of cooking, milling, fermentation, and distillation, essentially creating fine-grained distinctions where there had been none. Not surprisingly, no one wanted their mezcal branded as industrial, with the result that the category was streamlined to simply "mezcal" by the time the changes went into effect in April 2017 (see table 2.1).

The new categories were intended to give consumers more precise information about how their mezcal is made while potentially incentivizing makers who hewed to more labor-intensive or costly methods associated with making "artisanal" or "ancestral" mezcal. In practice, the changes created what some saw as artificial and arbitrary classifications for what had previously been labeled under a single name. For instance, "ancestral" mezcal requires roasted agave to be crushed using only wooden mallets or a wheel mill (variously called a *tahona,* Chilean mill, or Egyptian mill), whereas the agave for "artisanal" mezcal can be crushed using wood mallets, wheel mill, cane press, or chipper. Similarly, ancestral mezcal is characterized by a more limited range of acceptable "premodern" materials and technologies for other aspects of production, particularly distillation, which specifies the use of clay pots.

The differences between the categories may seem inconsequential to the uninitiated; mezcal was mezcal, after all, made from 100 percent agave regardless of categorization. But to those most invested in maintaining mezcal's craft distillate profile, the use of mechanical devices such as a chipper/shredder (known as a *hebradora* or *desgarradora* in Spanish), for example, was antithetical to that mission. Olson fell into that latter camp. He continued,

> I'm so happy that they're doing it [revising the DO for mezcal], because we need it, but I'm so disappointed at how far they fell short from the mark. The fact that we can use a wood chipper and still call it mezcal and artisanal, are you kidding me? Because you have guys that have been doing it for a while and for some reason we have to let them in! And yet, we can't allow alembic stills into the ancestral category because they're copper. It's like, they're five hundred years old! But a wood chipper, there's nothing artisanal about that. A *desgarradora* is basically a minidiffuser. It's unacceptable.

Mechanical shredders were a thorny issue all around, and Olson's comparison to a diffuser—an efficient but much derided mechanical device

Table 2.1 Norma Oficial Mexicana NOM-070-SCFI-2016, Bebidas alcohólicas-Mezcal-Especificaciones: New Categorizations, 2017.

	Mezcal	Artisanal Mezcal	Ancestral Mezcal
Cooking	Agave hearts or juice may be cooked in underground pits, above-ground masonry ovens, or autoclaves.	Agave hearts must be cooked in underground pits or above-ground masonry ovens.	Agave hearts must be cooked in underground, earthen pits.
Milling	Cooked agave may be crushed by *tahona*, Chilean/Egyptian mill, cane press, chipper, or roller mills.	Cooked agave may be crushed by wooden mallet, *tahona*, Chilean/Egyptian mill, cane press, or chipper.	Cooked agave can only be crushed using wooden mallets, *tahona*, or a Chilean/Egyptian mill.
Fermentation	Fermentation may take place in wooden, concrete, or stainless steel vats.	Fermentation can take place in rock pits, in-ground pits, tree trunks, clay urns, wooden vats, or animal hides; process may include agave fibers.	Fermentation can take place in rock pits, in-ground pits, tree trunks, masonry tanks, clay urns, wooden vats, or animal hides; process may include agave fibers.
Distillation	Distillation in alembic (pot) still or column (continuous) still made from copper or stainless steel.	Stills must be fueled by direct fire beneath a boiler of either copper or clay; the head or "hat" of the still may be made of clay, wood, copper, or stainless steel.	Stills must be fueled by direct fire with boilers constructed of clay, with the head or "hat" of the still constructed of clay or wood.

Source: Adapted from Terrazas (2017).

used in industrial tequila production—was particularly damning.[3] Admittedly, I was perplexed by the whole classification system. During my conversation with Olson I wondered aloud exactly who or what were the ancestors referenced by "ancestral" mezcal: was ancestral mezcal not "artisanal" mezcal and vice versa? "Exactly," he said.

Yet not everyone was bothered by these distinctions. Producers themselves were primarily concerned with meeting certification guidelines that would allow them to get their product into the market in the first place. Among these producers were beneficiaries of a short-term state government program under Oaxaca governor Gabino Cué Monteagudo that provided "kits" to small producers with the aim of helping them commercialize their mezcal. The kits contained a variety of equipment such as new stainless steel tanks, thermometers, scales, tarps, and hydrometers, as well as the aforementioned mechanical shredders. The producers I met who received the kits were generally grateful for the new equipment, having operated for decades with virtually no outside support. Even in cases when the technology was unfamiliar to them, there was a curiosity and willingness to learn, aided in part by state-funded workshops and classes. For instance, I participated in one workshop in which producers were taught how to use hydrometers to measure the percentage of alcohol by volume (ABV). The simple but effective tool could potentially provide a more accurate reading than the traditional method, which involves using a *carrizo* (reed) tube to produce *perlas*, or "pearls," little bubbles that form on top of mezcal when it is agitated (if the ABV is too high or low, the bubbles will quickly dissipate) (see figures 2.3 and 2.4).

This is not to say that small producers were about to abandon the techniques that ostensibly defined their mezcal as craft in the first place. Félix Ángeles Arellanes, a producer from Santa Catarina Minas who gained notoriety for his clay pot–distilled mezcal, was among those who received a mechanical shredder. When I visited his *palenque* one afternoon, I observed two young male workers crushing agave using large, wooden *mazos* (mallets) in an in-ground dugout known as a *canoa* for its canoe-like shape. Not far from there stood the *hebradora de agave*, which Félix fired up to give me a demonstration of how it worked. Notably, he did not seem at all conflicted about having this "modern" technology side by side with more "primitive" tools, his pragmatism trumping any philosophical concerns about the integrity of the craft. I asked him whether the mechanical shredder caused the finished mezcal to taste different from the mezcal whose agave had been pounded with mallets.

Figure 2.3 Del Maguey founder Ron Cooper demonstrates the traditional method of measuring ABV, using a *carrizo* tube and gourd bowl to produce "pearls." Photo by author.

Figure 2.4 A workshop where mezcal producers are taught to measure ABV using a hydrometer. Photo by author.

He said that he could not detect a qualitative difference. But he mentioned that some of his foreign clients with more purist leanings insisted it would compromise the flavor.

Indeed, many small producers are finding themselves faced by increased, and sometimes conflicting, demands on their craft as they enter the commercial market. Some have expressed concern about the ability to scale up while maintaining traditional production methods, especially given the nuances of the newest categories. A producer I interviewed told me that one of the beautiful things about craft mezcal was that no two batches were ever the same, even when made by the same person under relatively similar conditions. But this can prove a Catch-22. The craft imaginary may allow for some variability among its products—after all, they are handmade—but there is a limit to how much deviation consumers will tolerate. In the case of mezcal, some form of standardization is inevitable once a product hits the market, whether it be in the properties of the drink itself or in its packaging. Despite the intent of the market to embrace craft with all its variation and imperfections, the market is also the very thing that demands that craft products become bureaucratized and commoditized.

At the same time, the very nature of craft mezcal means that it does not always align with its curated, consummately Instagrammable ideal. Consumers express a desire for authenticity but may be ambivalent when confronted with authenticity of craft in all its messiness. For instance, one reality of crushing agave using a *tahona* is that the horse pulling the millstone will often defecate while it is working, occasionally spreading excrement among the mash that is to be fermented. Ultimately the waste is removed through the distillation process, but that does not prevent uninitiated onlookers, often tourists, from feeling disgust when a horse relieves itself in the raw materials of the craft mezcal they are there to consume. To this point, I once participated in a multiday course on mezcal certification in which the instructor suggested using an improvised horse diaper to create a more "hygienic" production environment. This elicited much laughter from the producers in attendance, one of whom retorted, "No le voy a poner un pinche pañal al caballo!" (I'm not going to put a fucking diaper on the horse!). More recently, Del Maguey issued a voluntary recall of *copitas* (small ceramic drinking cups) that it had widely distributed to customers at retail outlets, events, and tastings, due to high lead content (US FDA 2023). The company undoubtedly made the responsible decision, but this occurrence is a stark reminder of an artisanal economy in which Mexican ceramicists, often women, are exposed to toxic materials in their everyday work environment (Pérez 2019).

At a deeper level, all these examples point to a larger social unease residing within the current craft imaginary, as well as to the way that informal and formal systems of distinction emerge around a particular product. Authenticity in the twenty-first-century marketplace has become a cliché, and the categories we impose on the things we consume frustrate people because we often know or intuit that they are not really "authentic," no matter how much we will them to be. But what are the forces making these distinctive categories important in the first place? Why go to all the effort to make sure champagne is still champagne, or that mezcal is mezcal (ancestral, artisanal, or otherwise)? The reason people are so caught up with this distinctiveness is related to what they believe to be at stake, which is the belief that humans can shape their own destiny. This is true both for those who recoil at the thought of a wood chipper being used to make artisanal mezcal, and for the Indigenous producer who refuses to sell his artisanal mezcal to the tequila dealer at a cut-rate price. The craft imaginary permitted something that was previously devalued to be transformed into something of value; the market flipped, and it changed how people thought about their place and livelihoods in the world.

Critically, these categories are a proxy for discourse on sustainability and vulnerable communities, which may have significant impact, both positive and negative, on those who make these products. Consumers are asking for a more sustainable world, not only environmentally but socially, where the things they consume both simplify their lives and give them affirmation. In this way, the new craft imaginary mirrors previous moments in which craft held the promise of a more harmonious relationship between human labor and the material world. Yet we must account for the ways in which the market is making new demands on people and a product that have, at least in recent history, struggled to establish legitimacy. A producer can make mezcal all their life and do it well, and now they can purportedly prosper by doing so. Thus, we can say that the craft imaginary, and the market it represents, poses mezcal as a means for people to transform the way they are viewed in the world. However, to prosper the producer must understand all the complexities of the market's game, which are not dependent on any one group or individual: for every producer there is a consumer. As the producer meets the consumer on this newly created stage, it is worth examining what the consumer is doing as well. The next chapter looks at how the mythical narrative of craft mezcal is made and inculcated outside mezcal's traditional circuits of production and consumption.

3 | A Taste for Agave

> Pale silvery straw color. Aromas of cigar, roasted root vegetable, cucumber and delicate spice herbed rubbed pork with a silky, dryish medium body and a delicately smoky nut, cream, melon, and singed grass finish. Stylish and almost feminine.
>
> —Review of Wahaka brand Reposado con Gusano mezcal, Beverage Testing Institute

Descriptions like this one of Wahaka brand's mezcal *reposado con gusano* (barrel-aged mezcal flavored with maguey worms) are becoming more common as mezcal gains notoriety in national and international markets.[1] To the uninitiated, wine and spirits reviews may read as over-the-top, almost-nonsensical tributes or as mortifying disclaimers. But in the world of prestige beverages such as wine and Scotch whisky, comparisons to seemingly unrelated foods, mentions of nonedible flavors and aromas, and the attribution of anthropomorphic characteristics are de rigueur. That Oaxacan mezcal is now characterized in this fashion indicates that it has entered a particular regime of connoisseurship, one it was excluded from when it was a drink of mostly working-class and rural people and not yet "discovered" as an artisanal spirit.

In my more than a decade of studying mezcal, I attended tasting events in both the United States and Mexico, in restaurants, bars, fancy restaurants, and not-so-fancy restaurants, as well as in workshops and classes. The explicit aim of such events was always to educate participants about mezcal—in other words, to help them be better and more appreciative consumers. Yet while the process of cultivating mezcal expertise may be positively viewed, I found it in practice to be a potentially fraught activity. For instance, the first time I participated in a formal tasting, in Oaxaca City in 2011, I was instructed that the only mezcal worth drinking was artisanal, made from 100 percent agave, and never aged (i.e., one should only drink mezcal *joven* or *blanco*), as aging obscured the so-called pure flavors of the agave plant; the same rules of connoisseurship likewise dictated that a "good" mezcal should never be used for a cocktail. Ultimately, I found myself pushing back against such a purist approach, and when people asked me to recommend the best mezcal to drink, I would invariably reply, "The one that tastes good to you." More recently, I have found such strict gatekeeping by mezcal "experts" to be mitigated somewhat by the growing public interest in the drink.

But just why did people need coaching to learn to appreciate mezcal in the first place? Mezcal has been popular locally in Oaxaca for several hundred years, without the elaborate educational apparatus of tasting notes, tours, and descriptions of its production process. As noted here and elsewhere (Bowen 2015), extensive capital investment, certification procedures, regulatory commissions, protected geographic indications, and clever branding campaigns all helped bring mezcal to international markets, expanding its consumer base. However, the cultivation of a taste for mezcal in the twenty-first-century marketplace also relies on the drink's interdiscursivity to create new frameworks of connoisseurship for those who were not traditionally or historically its intended consumers. Defined as "the use of elements in one discourse and social practice which carry institutional and social meanings from other discourses and social practices" (Candlin and Maley 1997, 212), interdiscursivity encourages us to think through how certain symbolic and material practices associated with connoisseurship in one realm provide the terms for evaluating taste and value in another.

This chapter utilizes the concept of interdiscursivity to examine how tastemaking practices borrowed from other foods and beverages make mezcal legible or relatable outside of its original contexts of production and consumption. Highlighting mezcal's rarified qualities as signaled by particular renderings of craft provides a framework that not only makes the drink legible but also adds value for consumers. The examples supporting mezcal's transition from regional to national and international markets also point to the repositioning of mezcal within the racial and class politics that underlie Oaxaca's broader development as a "foodie" destination (Johnston and Baumann 2014). Emergent mezcal connoisseurship is directly related to the wider phenomenon of culinary cosmopolitanism, defined by sociologists Josée Johnston and Shyon Baumann (2014, 94) as "the desire to seek and experience the cuisines of the Exotic Other" (see also Heldke 2003). I contend that just as cosmopolitans have a "reputation for being [simultaneously] open-minded and elite" when it comes to gastronomy (Cappeliez and Johnston 2013), mezcal connoisseurship is inescapably rooted in social taste hierarchies, even as it purports to transcend them. This ultimately has ramifications for everyone along the mezcal value chain—producers, middlemen, and Mexican and non-Mexican consumers alike—as connoisseurship becomes an important mechanism in determining mezcal products' economic value in this still-emerging market.

Acquiring Taste and Value

As with other forms of alcohol, mezcal might be best described as an "acquired taste." Indeed, the US author of the blog *Mezcal PhD* (which at one point featured the tagline "an MBA in finance, but a PhD in Mezcal") notes that "there is a saying in the mezcal world that goes . . . 'mezcal is an acquired taste, but a taste worth acquiring'" (McEvoy 2013). This presumption of acquisition refers not only to the process of learning to enjoy mezcal as a sensorial experience but also to that of understanding the consumption of mezcal as a thoroughly social act. A novice must learn to enjoy the burning sensation of mezcal as it passes through the throat—in part a function of its high alcohol by volume (ABV)—and must come to appreciate the oft-present aroma and taste of wood smoke and the flavors of agave varietals utilized in its manufacture.[2] On this same note, when confronted with a mezcal distilled in a clay pot rather than a metal still, newcomers may not know what to make of its slightly viscous mouthfeel or its often-funky aromas, which for some evoke wet earth or cheese. Nevertheless, this individual sensorial experience is always embedded in a wider sociocultural context. As such, the process by which one actually acquires a taste for agave distillates such as mezcal or tequila may vary.

In the United States, tequila often serves as a baseline reference point for those new to mezcal, with many drinkers having tried a margarita cocktail or downed a shot of tequila at some point. It is thus not uncommon to hear mezcal likened to "smoky" or "spicy" tequila as a way of providing context for a first-time mezcal drinker. The experience of the liquor will differ for someone who has grown up in a Oaxacan community, where mezcal is regularly consumed in ritual or other social contexts, versus for someone whose first encounter with mezcal was at, say, a swanky cocktail bar in New York City. Certainly, the history of mezcal consumption in urban and rural Oaxacan settings is long and varied, worthy of study in its own right (see Vera Cortés and Fernández 2015). However, considering that the United States is currently mezcal's largest market, outpacing even its home country of Mexico (Coss

2022), more and more mezcal consumers come from backgrounds where mezcal is *not* traditionally present. How, then, does one learn to "appreciate" mezcal when the historical or cultural context associated with it is virtually absent?

In the case of mezcal, we like to think that our individual palates are enough to allow us to distinguish what tastes "good" from what does not. But in fact, mezcal is emblematic of how drinks as embodied semiotic and material forms both mediate and are mediated by social life (Manning 2012). Pierre Bourdieu (1984) theorized consumer choice as reflecting a symbolic hierarchy that is determined and maintained by the socially dominant in order to distinguish themselves from other classes of society. Using the consumption preferences of middle-class French society, Bourdieu argued that there is no such thing as pure, individual "taste"; all our aesthetic choices, from the clothes we wear to the foods and music we consume, are really forms of distinction. Moreover, these "judgments of taste" are an expression of social class formations in modern society—the tastes of one class are formed in opposition to those tastes that characterize other social classes.

For instance, wine is subject to a social organization of value-determining connoisseurship. Someone who has yet to appreciate a wine's subtleties has also yet to be accepted as part of the recognized social stratum in which the drink is regularly consumed and appreciated. Conversely, if a socially prominent wine drinker learns to appreciate a liquor made primarily by poor rural or working-class people, such as mezcal, then the liquor can be elevated: the socially prominent individual has the language to describe and, thereby, elevate the liquor; and the attraction of the exotic Other enhances the chance that the socially prominent individual will try the liquor and learn to appreciate it.

Linguistic anthropologist Michael Silverstein (2006, 484) shows how language mediates the relationship between humans and the wine they create as both an agricultural and aesthetic commodity. Through what he terms "oinoglossic registers," or more simply "wine-talk," social relationality is "mediated not directly by wine in its physicochemical or even directly sensorial presence, so much as by the discursive processes of representation of [wine]." Silverstein likens the speech acts associated with wine connoisseurship to other realms where demonstrating expertise is requisite for appreciation. As with European painting or period furniture, "wine-talk" reveals a structure of authority in which the judgments of "experts" are collectively agreed on as a basis for subsequent opinions or judgments by others. In this form of interdiscursivity, one quotes, cites, or alludes to authority in orienting oneself to the object of aesthetic judgment (Silverstein 2006, 483). In the case of wine, the "proper" authorities may include sommeliers, chefs, or fellow wine aficionados. Referencing numerical rating systems used by publications such as *Wine Enthusiast, Wine Spectator,* and *Wine Advocate* is one way to appeal to higher authority in crafting one's own expertise—and not surprisingly a strategy used by retail stores to entice people to buy the product.

The study of material objects has been central to anthropology since the discipline's inception. But whereas early anthropologists theorized objects as either "gifts" or commodities exchanged under highly circumscribed conditions, subsequent generations of scholars argued for analyzing what Arjun Appadurai (1986) called the "social life of things." As Igor Kopytoff (1986, 73) notes in the same volume, "commoditization is best looked upon as a process of becoming rather than as an all-or-none state of being." This position is key to understanding the enrichment economy, where wine has become a drinkable commodity that is subject to a host of value-creating judgments at every stage. Beginning as an agricultural product, the wine grape is transformed into a prestige consumer good (wine) through a complex value-creation chain (see Black and Ulin 2013). In this value regime, wine is recognized as,

> the emergent product of refined, sometimes "boutique" agricultural techniques . . . of growing, harvesting, pressing, vat or barrel fermenting, and bottling followed by distribution as at wholesale and retail levels, reaching consumers as a measured, packaged, labeled substance with a history and even a future bound up with numbers: bottle volume in standard sizes, year of vintage (harvesting and final release), quantity of production, number of exemplars still in commodity circulation at any given moment, etc. (Silverstein 2006, 483)

Silverstein's description of this chain reveals that true connoisseurship relies not solely on one's taste buds but also on the mastery of highly specialized knowledge: vintage, grape varietals, growing regions, wine tasting notes, food pairings, the differences in stemware, and more. While any hobby or profession may have its own specialized knowledge/language, Bourdieu reminds us that not all of these knowledges/languages are created equal. The interdiscursivity and exclusivity that Silverstein associates with "wine-speak" transcend the world of wine. They function within and across different classes of prestige food and drinks, including mezcal.

From Banal to Boutique

Not all the mezcals consumed as part of the global boom are what might be termed artisanal or boutique spirits. Market segmentation exists and is, arguably, necessary to elevating mezcal's social and economic value. Oaxacan mezcal today constitutes a range of products, including noncommercial mezcal produced for consumption within households or communities of origin as well as relatively inexpensive, commercial brands (e.g., Oro de Oaxaca and Monte Alban) that have been available for decades both within and outside of Mexico—what I have heard disparagingly referred to as "airport mezcal" for their seemingly wide availability (they can be picked up as an afterthought) and lower price point.[3] In contrast to these, the mezcal that *New York Times* food writer and critic Eric Asimov described in 2010 as "tequila's smoky, spicy cousin" and the "Next Big Thing" in the spirits world might be best classified as "third wave," a term used in the coffee industry to elevate a type of coffee as artisanal product rather than foodstuff or commodity.

Indeed, mezcal's trajectory is not wholly unlike coffee's historical transformation from mass drink into specialty product. Anthropologist William Roseberry (1996) described coffee's transformation into a "yuppie" drink in the American market beginning in the 1960s and continuing into the 1980s and 1990s. Second-wave coffee pioneers Peet's Coffee and Starbucks provided US consumers with an expanded coffee repertoire that included new varieties, roasts, and preparations. Knowing the difference between arabica and robusta beans, light and dark roasts, and such preparations as macchiato, Americano, and espresso became a way in which one could distinguish oneself from Folgers and Maxwell House drinkers. The more recent third-wave coffee movement, in turn, prizes artisanal coffee, emphasizing small-batch or microlot beans that have distinctive tastes tied to particular terroirs, exemplified on the national level by brands such as Counter Culture and Intelligentsia (Smith 2018). Additionally, it often takes up various social, economic, and environmental causes associated with coffee production. An ethos of product authenticity and sustainability is critical to such brands, even those that have a national reach—signaled by such buzzwords as "Fair Trade" and "bird friendly"—making coffee an ideal case study for scholars interested in ethical consumerism (Cailleba and Casteran 2010).

But others have taken a still more critical stance on third-wave coffee and the value signaled through ideologies of place-based production and limited supply. In his study of third-wave coffee production in the Guatemala Highlands, Edward F. Fischer (2022, 12) observes that "roasters, baristas, and marketers—as well as the growing number of passionate amateurs and aficionados—play an active role in defining what quality is, how a *different* taste becomes a *more valued* taste." Yet the surplus value created through the third-wave narrative actually remains overwhelmingly in the hands of distributors rather than Indigenous Maya coffee farmers. The producers may have control over the land and means of production, but the "largest percentage of economic value extracted from the rarified prices of Third Wave coffee comes not from control over terroir but [from] translating the material quality of the beans into the symbolic and imaginative narratives of affluent consumers" (Fischer 2022, 12–13). Sarah Bowen (2015) has advanced a similar argument for Mexican agave spirits. She convincingly shows how those on the production end of the mezcal and tequila supply chain, including agave harvesters and small-scale distillate producers, stand to gain very little from national and international certifications that supposedly protect and guarantee the quality of the regionally based product.

Setting aside for a moment the question of inequity fostered by the third-wave lexicon, I would point out how it contributes to a value-added framework that operates in an interdiscursive mode with other classes of specialty products. The "bean-to-bar" chocolate model, for example, relies on the traceability of a raw material (cacao) to a particular national or regional location that supposedly imbues the finished product (chocolate) with a unique flavor profile (Schnepel 2002). Creo Chocolate, a company based in Portland, Oregon—a US city that has become synonymous with the craft food industries and agricultural transparency, to the point of parody in some cases (look no further than the television series *Portlandia*)—sources heirloom Arriba Nacional cacao from Ecuador. Creo Chocolate (n.d.) describes its chocolate in the following manner: "This is a handcrafted bar. We roast, crack, winnow, grind, conche, temper, mold, and package small batches of chocolate in our factory and tasting room. Our cacao beans are sourced directly from the farmer and crafted to bring out their interesting flavors." Embracing an ethos of environmental sustainability, the company also participates in the Heirloom Cacao Preservation Fund, a US nonprofit organization whose mission is to "save the quickly diminishing *Theobroma cacao* trees that produce the most high quality, flavorful chocolate and identify the farmers who grow them" (Heirloom Cacao, n.d.).

Such specialized language, whether it is of the "wine-talk," third-wave coffee, or bean-to-bar chocolate variety, emphasizes commodity as craft and product traceability to particular lands or producers over other potential aesthetic or gustatory qualities. Similar elements are at work in the present-day mezcal industry. Indeed, an article in the *New Yorker* points out that "the mezcal boom coincides with the popularity of farm-to-table food, the rise of the craft cocktail, and the advent of the bartender as an advocate for environmental and social justice" (Goodyear 2016). *New Yorker* readers are an obvious target market in the United States for what I am terming "third-wave mezcal" because the magazine's primary readership includes well-educated, prosperous individuals who are extensively traveled and versed in contemporary political and cultural issues. These readers often dwell in major urban areas where mezcal is available or have the means to travel directly to the source in Oaxaca. More importantly, the mezcal boom does more than simply coincide with the farm-to-table, craft cocktail, and related artisanal food and beverage movements. The wider framework of "craft" discussed in the previous chapter is integral to an appreciation of mezcal: it is to be sipped, savored, debated, and evaluated through the same tasting mechanisms as wine and other well-known distillates such as cognac and Scotch whisky. Not surprisingly, traceability matters.

In 1994, in an attempt to regulate and legitimize mezcal, Mexico ratified the Norma Oficial Mexicana NOM-070-SCFI-1994, governing mezcal's denomination of origin (DO). This law laid out standards for mezcal's production, certification process, labeling, and regional classification system. Modeled on the French *appellation d'origine contrôlée* (AOC) used for wine and other agricultural products, a DO in Mexico is defined as "the name of a geographical region of a country that serves to designate a product originating therein, the qualities and characteristics of which are due exclusively to the geographical environment, including natural or human factors" (quoted in Bowen 2015, 66). As with tequila, which was first accorded geographic indicator/DO protection in Latin America in 1974, the mezcal DO from the beginning opened up a whole new place-based rhetoric of authenticity and heritage (Gaytán 2018). This rhetoric locates Oaxaca as an epicenter.

The conception of mezcal as a craft spirit was the driving force behind Del Maguey, a company founded in 1995 by Ron Cooper, a New Mexico–based artist. Cooper is generally credited as the first importer of artisanal mezcal to the US market (Greene 2017), where he introduced—and subsequently copyrighted—the idea of Del Maguey's "Single Village Mezcal." The phrase evokes single malt Scotch whisky, which is produced in Scotland in a pot still at a single distillery, with malted barley as the only grain ingredient. Unlike the commercial brands of mezcal available outside of Oaxaca in the mid-1990s, Del Maguey's Single Village Mezcal was ostensibly produced in one village, at one *palenque* (mezcal distillery), using one type of agave. Other artisanal brands emerged in the wake of Del Maguey, focusing on small-batch production from specific communities or families. Bottles of these mezcals generally start at around US$40 or US$50 but may cost upward of US$200 for a bottle distilled with *pechuga de conejo* (rabbit breast), like that sold by Pierde Almas, a company founded by another American artist now living in Mexico, Jonathan Barbieri.

While it seems simple enough from a marketing perspective, Del Maguey's model changed the playing field for mezcal in the United States. Consumers now had a conceptual framework for understanding mezcal in much the same way that they had come to appreciate the vast number of wines that were available to them. Cooper, unwittingly or not, had inserted the French concept of terroir, the "taste of place," into the mezcal world (Trubek 2009). Today, it is not uncommon to hear the Spanish term *terruño* (piece of land or native soil) used to describe mezcal. Location—soil conditions, altitude, temperature, water sources, and so on—is critical to third-wave mezcal's popularity. It is not enough to know that mezcal comes from Mexico or even a specific state such as Oaxaca; true mezcal connoisseurship relies on a deeper understanding of Oaxacan geography. Whereas outsider knowledge of Oaxaca was once largely limited to the state capital of Oaxaca City, its immediate environs, and coastal resorts, mezcal aficionados now have on their radar previously undetected regions (e.g., Miahuatlán and Sola de Vega) and the smaller communities they contain (e.g., San Luis Amatlán and Candelaria Yegolé).

Knowledge of terroir is only one aspect of the interdiscursivity that Silverstein identities with "wine-talk," and the same may be said of mezcal. From plant to product, mezcal authorities elevate the spirit's value through other specialized, yet highly profuse discourses. (Notably, these authorities tend to be distributors, marketers, and consumers or other boosters, rather than producers.) As with wine, third-wave mezcal holds the promise of unlimited sensorial and intellectual pursuit. In *Mezcal: The History, Craft and Cocktails of the World's Ultimate Artisanal Spirit*, Emma Janzen (2017, 11) describes mezcal as "wild and free and (almost totally) unrestricted" in terms of its production details, adding that its appreciation requires "a more cerebral sense." Janzen's characterization of mezcal contrasts sharply with its previous image as a harsh, hangover-inducing drink. She instructs the reader that a desirable mezcal should be bottled to let "a mix of many flavors [come] to a balance," allowing for the "soft flavor of mezcal" to come through (106, 134). Drawing on the allure of both cocktail culture and *terruño*, she also waxes poetic about how the same cocktail will taste completely different depending on the region that produced the mezcal.

Nowhere is the enumeration of mezcal's "boutique agricultural techniques" (Silverstein 2006) and production methods more clearly demonstrated than in the current generation of bottle labels. Take, for example, the labeling of Mezcalosfera, the export brand from Mezcaloteca, an appointment-only tasting room in the city of Oaxaca that bills itself as "a project dedicated to the diffusion and conservation of Mexico's traditional mezcal and its diverse biocultural processes" (Mezcaloteca, n.d.). The details gathered on the label of one bottle of Mezcaloteca purchased on-site in Oaxaca (my translation) read:

Tobalá/Madrecuixe

master mezcal maker	Felipe Cortés
state	Oaxaca
town	Miahuatlán
maguey utilized	*A. potatorum* 50 percent, *A. karwinskii* 50 percent
maguey altitude	1560–2100 meters above sea level
oven type	conical in-ground pit
wood used	mesquite and oak
grinding method	stone wheel
type of fermentation vat	ashe juniper
fermentation	wild yeast
water used for fermentation	spring water
fermentation time	7 days
number of distillations	2
type of still	copper with condenser
dilution and blending	*puntas* [heads] and spring water
distillation date	August 2015
liters produced	220
lot number	01-15

Not all mezcal labels contain this level of production detail. Nevertheless, providing some combination of these descriptors has become standard labeling practice for artisanal mezcal. Importantly, third-wave mezcals typically include the name of the *maestro mezcalero* (master mezcal maker) who made them. Del Maguey founder Ron Cooper not only coined the expression "Single Village Mezcal," but is also strong in his conviction that mezcal's *terruño* is in part attributed to what he calls "the hand of the maker" (pers. comm. 2015). In other words, each bottle is essentially a work of craftsmanship that may be traced not only to a single location but to a single individual. In the same way that the signature of a well-known artist may add value to a piece of Oaxacan folk art, the name of the *maestro mezcalero*—or better yet, his actual signature on the bottle—adds value to the finished product.

While certain production elements are self-explanatory, such as the maker's name and the state or town of the mezcal's origin, other elements included on artisan mezcal labels demand higher-order connoisseurship for their legibility. Only the most educated of consumers, for instance, would recognize the scientific names *A. potatorum* and *A. karwinskii*, or their respective local names, tobalá and madrecuixe. Furthermore, both tobalá and madrecuixe are distinguished from the domesticated espadín (*A. angustifolia*), the most commonly used agave in Oaxacan mezcal production. Even though today tobalá and madrecruixe are not exclusively found and harvested in the wild, they are considered part of a class of what mezcal aficionados refer to as "wild" and "rare" agave varieties (traditionally harvested in the wild, now sometimes domesticated or propagated from wild agaves), some of which are allegedly in danger of extinction due to increasing demand. Mezcals made from these "wild" agaves are often perceived as more valuable as well as more complex or nuanced in taste. Fausto Zapata, cofounder of Mezcal El Silencio, lamented the "wild" trend to a US journalist, stating, "A lot of consumers who I talk to have become 'Tobalá drinkers only' or 'Tepeztate drinkers'" (Signer 2016). Not surprisingly, Mezcal El Silencio focuses primarily on espadín.

Part and parcel of the recent phenomenon in which mezcal aficionados profess knowledge of the subtleties of agave varietals is the emergence of mezcal *ensambles*. Unheard of a decade ago in the mezcal world, this Spanish term is akin to the English-language *blend* as applied to other wine and spirits categories; it means that two or more agave varieties have been distilled together in a single batch. From the connoisseur's perspective, a successful mezcal *ensamble* strikes a harmonious balance between the unique characteristics of each agave variety used in the blend. For example, the following review of a four-agave *ensamble* by Oaxaca-based mezcal brand Koch hints that blending is the redeeming quality of an otherwise ho-hum mezcal: "Much like with cognac, blending is at the heart of this mezcal. Utilizing four different wild and rare species of agave the blender is looking to heighten the drinking experience by keying up certain strengths and balancing out any shortcomings this mezcal might have. Cirial adds spice and earthiness while Tobalá adds body and sweetness. Lumbre brightens and Tobasiche provides depth and herbal characteristics" (Distiller, n.d.).

Yet mezcal connoisseurship does not end with being able to discern between agave varieties and knowing how to blend them. As the long list of information from the label above suggests, different types of materials utilized at various stages of the production process also contribute to mezcal's endless range of flavors and aromas. Thus, mezcal made in a copper still with a serpentine condenser has a different flavor profile than mezcal made in a clay pot still; indeed, the latter is considered to be more rustic technology and is now classified as "ancestral" mezcal according to the most recent criteria for the DO. As with wine or whiskey, the materials that make up the vats used for fermentation and aging (French or American oak, juniper, etc.) add another layer of flavor that may be detectable by connoisseurs. With so many variables affecting the taste of the final product, it is not difficult to see why mezcal has been characterized as a drink of infinite possibilities (Starkman 2021).

This brings us back to the question of how a drink sometimes described as "gut rot" by detractors is now seen as a complex drink possessing aromas of "fresh cotton, chick peas, and slate," as one online reviewer described Del Maguey's Wild Papalome (Jonny, comment on Mezcal Reviews, n.d.b.). Mezcal's rise is analogous to Oaxaca's transformation from a poor, backwater region of Mexico to a trendy destination for art and food lovers. While much of the state remains economically marginalized, cosmopolitan consumers have reframed certain aspects of Oaxaca's traditional agricultural goods and its corresponding craft-based market economy (S. Cook and Diskin 1975). This reframing operates within a global movement that elevates the economic and social value of artisanal production; such concepts as farm-to-table, bean-to-bar, and third wave, while not typically applied to mezcal, support a new framework of value creation based on certain modes of production and traceability to a geographic territory and its people. Within this reframing, the historical underdevelopment or noncommercialization of key Oaxacan industries is precisely what has allowed those same industries to flourish in the new global context. Craft—what once allowed Oaxacan mezcal to languish while tequila rose to fame—is now the word of the moment and a seemingly value-added component of much mezcal.

This chapter has shown how a cosmopolitan consumer class creates mezcal's value through interdiscursive means, taking elements from the discourse and social practices of wine appreciation and other forms of gastronomic connoisseurship. Ten years ago, it would have been unheard of to find a foreigner in Oaxaca searching for a tobasiche mezcal from Ejutla de Crespo in the same way that one might make a pilgrimage to Islay to sample a particular Scotch whisky. Like Silverstein's "wine-talk," the current mezcal-talk has opened up new markets and avenues for the cultural appreciation of Oaxaca. In other words, a product and a place that have long existed have been "enriched" for a certain type of consumer. Indeed, at a 2018 tasting event in Albuquerque, New Mexico, Clayton Szczech, an agave spirits entrepreneur, educator, and author, commented that US consumers were learning to enjoy mezcal the way they had learned to enjoy wine, but perhaps without the same pretension. Laughing, he said, "People always tell me, 'You guys are just like the wine people, except you're not snobs.'" But as we know, in the case of wine, chocolate, and other craft foodstuffs, newfound appreciation often comes with a high price tag. The market segmentation that we have seen with wine, chocolate, coffee, and mezcal provides opportunities for new realms of connoisseurship, but at what price?

4 | Mezcal, Mole, and Oaxaca Tourism

Oaxacan singer Lila Downs is internationally known for her evocative songs that put a modern spin on traditional Mexican sounds and motifs, and her 2006 hit song "La Cumbia del Mole" is no exception. It narrates local folklore and foodways to the rhythm of a traditional *cumbia* beat, accompanied by an eclectic mix of electric guitar, accordion, clarinet, and harp. The lyrics transport listeners to Oaxaca, where the people take their coffee with mezcal and local herbs are invoked as a remedy for wickedness. In this dreamscape, a Oaxacan woman nearby lovingly begins to prepare a mole, the iconic Mexican dish that typically includes a variety of ground chiles, chocolate, nuts, and spices.

Long a pop cultural ambassador for her natal region, Downs expanded that role in 2014, when she became the spokesperson for the Oaxacan Secretariat of Tourism and Economic Development's advertising campaign "Ven a Oaxaca, tienes que vivirlo!" (Come to Oaxaca, you have to live it!). For anyone in Oaxaca City that year, it was hard to miss, from images plastered on city walls and buses to local television ads. An extended promotional video, over four minutes in length, featured an opening scene of Downs draped in a heavy woolen serape, singing her way through an agave field and small *palenque* (mezcal distillery) before making her way to the spectacular ruins of a Monte Albán magically empty of tourists (see Vive Oaxaca 2014). Along the way she tries her hand at cutting the fronds off a spiky agave plant with a machete and helps load the cut agave hearts into a pit for roasting, all the while accompanied by a kindly Oaxacan *mezcalero* (mezcal maker), with whom she eventually raises a shot glass of the finished libation in a celebratory toast.

That the state government enlisted Downs to boost its public profile comes as no surprise, as she is a natural mediator of an emerging Oaxaca brand. Her music and persona have always appealed to national and international audiences, and arguably she is just as popular outside of Mexico as she is with Mexicans. One might even say that the singer embodies the present-day spirit of Oaxacan tourism itself. Since her first album in 1994, she has been known for her multilingual music, sung not only in Spanish and English, but also in Mixtec and Zapotec, two of Oaxaca's numerous Indigenous languages. Her personal aesthetic is a modern, colorful pastiche that reinvents regional Indigenous design and dress, calling to mind a modern-day Frida Kahlo. Moreover, Downs's music has been a booster for iconic Mexican food and drink, specifically mole, mezcal, and chocolate.[1] "La Cumbia del Mole" remains one of Downs's best-known songs, while the albums *Bullets and Chocolate* (2015) and *La Cantina* (2006) pay homage to another of Oaxaca's iconic foods and popular Mexican drinking culture, respectively ("La Cumbia del Mole" appears on the latter album). While not exclusive to Oaxaca, the triumvirate of mole, mezcal, and chocolate now serves as a powerful shorthand for the region's complex gastronomy turned tourist attraction.

Today it is less of a novelty to saunter through agave fields and visit a working mezcal distillery, but this sort of tourist activity would have been anomalous in the not-so-distant past. At the start of the twenty-first century, most tourist visits to a *palenque* occurred as part of package day trips from Oaxaca City. More often than not, such visits took place at small distilleries along the Pan-American Highway east of the city or in the town of Santiago Matatlán, where visitors were offered inexpensive mezcal at roadside storefronts. Tourists could admire and photograph the massive stone used to grind the agave and down a shot or two before continuing on to other destinations. These roadside attractions may or may not have been actual working distilleries, but they were easy to access and helped tourists visualize aspects of the production process. Craft brewing, artisanal distilleries, the cocktail renaissance, and, most importantly, mezcal itself were not yet parts of mainstream culture in most places, and few tourists planned visits to Oaxaca to include an immersive mezcal experience.

This changed with the mezcal boom that began around 2010, when tourism arose in tandem with the growth of national and international markets for mezcal (García Garza 2021). Today, we find a tourist subculture that not only wants to drink mezcal, but wants to know exactly how it is made and by whom, and even wants to participate in the production process. Oaxaca City is the starting and ending point for many such tourists, offering a genteel arts and culture–based consumer experience, expanding in recent years to include Oaxacan gastronomy. In this chapter I focus on this burgeoning, highly specialized tourist sector and the elements that distinguish it from tourism found elsewhere, including in the Tequila region (previously discussed).

Oaxaca is not just another place; it is a place whose economy relies on intensely market-driven cultural tourism. On a broader level, this chapter locates tourism in relationship to what I call folkloric gentrification, a process by which folk and popular culture has been targeted by upscale marketing and development. Incidentally, Oaxacan scholar Abraham Nahón (2020) has coined an even more regionally specific term for this gentrification, *guelaguetzificación,* a play on the Guelaguetza, Oaxaca's largest folk performance, held annually in the state capital. Whichever term we use, year after year Oaxacan folk arts, festivals, and, importantly, food and drink are ever more visible, consumable, and curated. To wit: we see folkloric gentrification at work not only in the decision to hold part of the 2022 Mercedes-Benz Fashion Week Mexico in Oaxaca, but even more in the staging of the event, which had the fashion models traverse runways temporarily set up in a field of agaves. Ultimately, mezcal tourism cannot be separated from this process, as it enlists tourists with select "consumption skills and technologies" that actively co-create the tourist experience (Chabrol and Muchnik 2011), both of mezcal and of Oaxaca more generally. The place does not simply attract tourists; the tourists also make the place (see figure 4.1).

Becoming a Food and Drink Destination

In the summer of 2022 *Travel and Leisure* magazine named Oaxaca the number one city in the world to visit, singling it out for its culinary delights. To the magazine writers there was apparently no contest: "Boasting an endless supply of mezcal and mole, Oaxaca is undoubtedly one of the ultimate food and drink destinations on the planet" (Japhe 2022). Today it is rare to encounter depictions of Oaxaca that do not highlight its regional cuisine, from blogs and cookbooks to travel magazines and television shows. Where food once played a supporting role, it now takes center stage, and mezcal is an unequivocal star within this emerging gastronomic constellation. Oaxaca ticks just about every box of a twenty-first-century culinary zeitgeist that enthusiastically embraces

Figure 4.1 A banner hanging inside the main hall of Oaxaca City's airport terminal. Photo by author.

street food, craft beverages, farm-to-table, non-GMOs, and famous chefs. Because Oaxaca has become such a foodie destination, it is hard to imagine a time when the place was otherwise. Yet early tourism in Oaxaca, and in Mexico generally, was not primarily cuisine driven. That is to say that food and drink were incidental to the tourist experience rather than integral. To understand the dynamics of today's mezcal tourism, then, we must situate it within national tourism and the niche occupied by Oaxaca within Mexico as the country took its place among the top ten tourist destinations in the world.

Historian Dina Berger (2006) traces the emergence of the modern Mexican tourism industry to the late 1920s, noting that the Mexican state began to promote travel in an effort to rebuild Mexico's tattered economy and image abroad after the 1910–1920 Mexican Revolution. American motor tourists, in particular, were encouraged by the creation of new highways, roadside hotels, and restaurants, and by the 1930s they were more willing than ever to drive south of the border to sightsee. From 1925 to 1937, Mexico completed a stretch of roadway down the eastern side of the country, from Laredo, Texas, all the way to Mexico City; it would ultimately become part of the Pan-American Highway. Berger (2006, 2) notes that in a relatively short period, Mexico's "vast beaches, curative waters, Mesoamerican pyramids, Indian villages and markets, colonial buildings, Porfirian monuments and boulevards, and modern constructs" were transformed into easily accessible sights and destinations. Ease of highway travel was complemented by a favorable exchange rate, pleasant weather, and a burgeoning popular media touting Mexico's historical and cultural richness. By the 1940s, Mexico, along with France and Canada, was one of the top foreign destinations for US travelers.

Yet for all their curiosity and willingness to explore, Americans were apparently more inclined to see the local *fondas* (inexpensive restaurants) and marketplaces as food for the eyes than for the stomach. Early guidebooks reinforced this. Folklorist Frances Toor's *Motorist Guide to Mexico* (1938), for example, described the weekly market in Pátzcuaro, Michoacán, as "one of the most picturesque and interesting markets in Mexico," but did not offer any suggestions on what to sample among its diverse foodstuffs (quoted in Jolly 2018, 106). Berger (2006) characterizes these early US travelers, who had recently lived through Prohibition (1920–1933), as in search of "pyramids by day, martinis by night." In other words, their tolerance for the exotic and unfamiliar did not necessarily extend to their eating and drinking habits, which fell back on options familiar to the American middle- and upper-class palate. Jeffrey M. Pilcher (2010), for instance, describes how the gold standard of tourist fare in Mexico City was Sanborns, a chain of department stores and diner-style restaurants brought to Mexico by entrepreneurial Californians Walter and Frank Sanborn. At Sanborns, chefs "greeted North American travelers with familiar hot cakes and ice cream sodas in addition to a nonthreatening selection of Mexican cuisine, including their signature dish, *enchiladas suizas* (Swiss enchiladas) topped with cream and cheese" (Pilcher 2010, 229). Diners who worried about sanitation were assured that not only did Sanborns use purified water in its kitchens, but it sourced its milk from its own herd of certified Jersey cows.

Even as Mexico City became a popular destination for modern travelers, Oaxaca tourism in the first half of the twentieth century was more circumscribed, for many of the same reasons that its mezcal industry remained localized. The state's geographic location—far to the south, amid formidable mountain ranges—made it less accessible than other parts of Mexico. Endemic poverty and lack of "modern" conveniences also proved obstacles to the sort of commercial tourism developing in Mexico City and coastal resort cities like Acapulco and Puerto Vallarta, and that included in the choice of food offerings. Thus, early travelers to Oaxaca were often of a more bohemian persuasion: artists, writers, and intellectuals with socialist leanings who found inspiration in its colorful traditions and well-preserved Indigenous communities. Over time,

Oaxaca's reputation as off the beaten path made it a desirable destination for the backpacker set of the 1960s and 1970s North American counterculture. The *jipis* (hippies), as they were called in Spanish, demonstrated their own utopian leanings. However, traveling on a shoestring budget, they were in search of neither sanitized (à la Sanborns) nor "gourmet" versions of local cuisine. If anything, the edible that attracted the most attention was Oaxaca's hallucinogenic mushrooms, popularized by Indigenous Mazatec healer María Sabina (Feinberg 2003). She allowed tourist outsiders to take part in psychedelic ceremonies, only to later regret that decision when she faced sharp criticism from some in her community. This is not to say that the *jipis* who made their way to Oaxaca did not appreciate the local foods they encountered. The 1960s and 1970s saw the rise of US "countercuisine" (Belasco 2006), in which minimally processed, plant-based foods such as granola, herbal tea, and soy products were embraced in defiance of an increasingly industrialized food system—and as highly profitable markets. Thus, Oaxaca's traditional markets, overflowing with unpasteurized, fresh cheese, *chapulines* (grasshoppers), and freshly ground pastes for making mole, aligned with a countercultural ideology of a return to a more natural diet, precursors to today's organic and farm-to-table movements.

At the same time, the concept of a global palate was starting to infiltrate the culinary mainstream back in the United States. Already primed by a decade of French cooking via Julia Child's television show *The French Chef* (filmed from 1963 to 1973), adventurous home cooks signed up for ethnic cooking classes and experimented with Chinese, Indian, and other "exotic" non-European ingredients and techniques. The 1972 publication of *The Cuisines of Mexico* by the late culinary doyenne Diana Kennedy was a defining moment in the trend toward Mexican food, marking the advent of a preoccupation with authentic, regional food preparation by English-speaking cooks. Ignacio M. Sánchez Prado (2020, 569) notes that the narrative of authenticity pioneered by Kennedy and chefs and food writers following in her footsteps, including chef and restaurateur Rick Bayless, "has been central in diversifying Mexican food within the United States and in revaluing it within Mexico itself." But it is not just Mexican cuisine in general that has been elevated; specific regions of Mexico are subject to much more attention than others. Browsing through *The Cuisines of Mexico* and Kennedy's subsequent books, one is struck by the multiple references to Oaxaca, whether to dishes she sampled in situ or those prepared by her Oaxacan domestic help. Kennedy's fascination with Oaxaca led her to eventually pen a massive, 464-page tome dedicated entirely to the state, *Oaxaca al gusto*, published first in Spanish (2008) and two years later in English (2010). In it, she characterizes Oaxaca as having one of Mexico's most diverse and exciting regional cuisines.

The culinary diversity that so impressed Kennedy was but one facet of Oaxaca's multiculturalism that set the stage for full-blown "ethnic tourism" to develop and thrive throughout the 1980s and 1990s. Describing a parallel industry in the neighboring state of Chiapas, sociologist Pierre L. Van den Berghe (1994, 9) has characterized ethnic tourism as travel in search of "unspoiled natives, not bilingual waiters and beach boys." Ethnic tourism in Oaxaca rested on the twin pillars of folk art and archaeology, primarily concentrated in Oaxaca City and the communities of the surrounding Central Valleys. No Oaxaca trip was complete without visiting the archaeological sites of Mitla and Monte Albán and artisan villages making wood carvings, pottery, and textiles (Brulotte 2012). Well-educated middle- and upper-class Europeans and North Americans interested in Mexican history and cultural heritage were one market. But so, too, was a growing Mexican middle class with the economic means for travel. Like all other emerging classes, this group took its lead from economically and socially mobile people from other places, particularly the United States.

Ethnic tourism still prevails in Oaxaca as it did through the 1980s and 1990s, but it has taken on new characteristics in the twenty-first century that mirror tourism trends globally. Notably, there is an emphasis on experiential tourism, in which individuals—no longer content with simply sightseeing—seek to create meaning and connections in their travels through direct experience (Salazar and Graburn 2014). Recreational and ecotourism in previously untouristed communities throughout the state have become more popular. A good example is the *pueblos mancomunados* (roughly translated as a commonwealth of villages), a group of eight Indigenous Zapotec communities in the Sierra Norte region that have combined resources to develop tourism infrastructure. In addition to the usual outdoor activities such as hiking, biking, zip-lining, and horseback riding, one of the towns, San Antonio Cuajimoloyas, has become the site of a popular annual wild mushroom festival that draws visitors from all over the world. Other Oaxacan communities have been host to volunteer tourism, premised on combining service activities in host communities with recreational and educational opportunities for participants (McGehee 2014; Mostafanezhad 2016). Finally, although often overlooked, a burgeoning wedding tourism industry has taken root, both in Oaxaca

City, with its gilded churches and restored colonial buildings, and on lush coastal resorts. These locations have become hot spots for destination weddings for affluent Mexicans and, increasingly, foreigners.

Among these developing sectors, however, it is gastronomy that has really put Oaxaca on the map as a global destination. To give some context for how much its food scene has changed: when I lived there as a student in 1995, ordering a cup of coffee in a café often meant getting a jar of Nescafé granules and hot water delivered to one's table. Travelers at the time obsessed about getting so-called Montezuma's revenge from an errant piece of ice floating in a drink. Like many foreigners, I had been cautioned to avoid eating food purchased from street vendors and market stalls, including the ubiquitous *quesillo*, an unpasteurized local cheese with the consistency of mozzarella. In contrast, street food has become a globally popular culinary genre, with its own dedicated tours, cookbooks, blogs, and television shows encouraging people to follow the locals. According to Jeffrey Pilcher (2010, 221), we should not be surprised by radical shifts in attitude toward food and consumption patterns. He writes, "Through food and drink, tourists from the United States have consumed their Mexican neighbors: alternately dominating, transforming, excluding, and embracing them according to an Orientalist logic that evolves with social relations in both countries."

In the current move from sightseeing to more experiential forms of tourism, food has emerged as "both a destination and a vehicle for tourism" (Long 2004, 2). Not only are travelers combining traditional leisure activities with food-related ones, they are increasingly structuring their entire trips around cooking, eating, and drinking. These new tourist mobilities are linked to the growth of an international food culture. Alyshia Gálvez (2018) argues that the North American Free Trade Agreement (NAFTA) and the neoliberal reforms of the 1990s intensified the commodification and appropriation of Mexican foodstuffs globally. For instance, more corn is now grown on industrial farms in the American Midwest than in Mexico, its agricultural birthplace. Meanwhile, Mexican food staples such as tortillas have turned into gastronomic amenities, made of organic, heirloom corn and forming the base of "craft" tacos worldwide. Critically, tourism is a key mechanism by which "many different people and institutions are involved in promoting and profiting from the boom in Mexican cuisine globally" (Gálvez 2018, 33).

Mexico is among the vanguard of the culinary tourism trend, especially since 2010, when it became one of the first countries in the world to secure a UNESCO Intangible Cultural Heritage designation for its cuisine. Heightening the visibility of Mexican food internationally, the designation became the impetus for a national branding campaign, including the creation of eighteen national "gastronomic routes" (*rutas gastronómicas*). These interstate byways connect and promote travel experiences through multiple culinary lenses, focusing on particular foods (cacao, vanilla), shared histories (the tristate mining region of Aguascalientes, San Luis Potosí, and Zacatecas), and traditions (Day of the Dead in the state of Michoacán). One route, the Ruta de los Mil Sabores de Mole (Route of a Thousand Flavors of Mole), purportedly covers three hundred variations of Mexico's famous dish across the states of Tlaxcala, Puebla, and Oaxaca (for the route map, see SECTUR, n.d.).

Already gaining traction as a gastronomic destination, Oaxaca has benefited from Mexico's moment in the UNESCO spotlight by launching its own food-related competitions, festivals, and other public events. A movement to promote Oaxacan *cocineras tradicionales* (traditional female cooks) has drawn attention to women as bearers of food traditions, turning them into living "cultural heritage" and tourist attractions in their own right (Hryciuk 2019; Matta 2019). Some efforts have been decidedly upscale, such as El Saber del Sabor (The Knowledge of Flavor), an annual festival highlighting Oaxacan cuisine that kicked off in 2009. It brings chefs from all over Mexico and the world and boasts sponsors such as *Food & Wine* magazine and the Mexico City branch of the famed Le Cordon Bleu cooking school. Add to that a new crop of cooking schools, market tours, and local "gastronomic fairs," honoring everything from regional moles and ice creams to *nicuatole*, a corn-based gelatinous sweet that is a popular street snack, and *tejate*, a pre-Hispanic beverage made from toasted corn, fermented cacao seeds, cacao flower, and seeds from the native mamey fruit. Even the humble empanada, whether stuffed with cheese and squash blossoms or with chicken and *mole amarillo* (yellow mole), has its own festival. In April 2019 the state government started planning a multimillion-dollar "gastronomic center" in the historic city center, with the goal of not only "rescuing traditional and indigenous Oaxacan cuisine" but also providing better tourist offerings in the downtown area (Oaxaca 2019). What foods need rescuing are not mentioned in the original plan, but the massive center, which now occupies a restored convent, is proof that food-centered tourism is there to stay. Mezcal tourism is clearly part of this increasingly commodified gastronomic landscape, summed up by one California tourist who told me, "I came for the mole and stayed for the mezcal." The sections that follow examine how the context for mezcal tourism took a distinct turn from tequila tourism, highlighting some of the geographic, economic, and social dimensions underlying it.

"Mezcal Is Not Tequila!"

I could not help but flinch when the state tourism official in Oaxaca City leaned across his office desk during our 2015 interview and passionately shook his finger at me. "I repeat, mezcal is not tequila, and it never will be!" I had obviously touched a nerve by asking whether he thought that mezcal was headed down the same touristic path as tequila. When further pushed, he acknowledged the success of tourism in the Tequila region, adding that mezcal tourism was "at least twenty years behind." At the same time, he insisted that the very nature of mezcal production in Oaxaca did not lend itself to the large-scale, corporate-driven tourism of tequila. "Mezcal is purer, less commercial," he stressed. He was referring not to the drinks' physical properties but rather to the notion of mezcal as sacrosanct, something whose very nature appealed to a more discerning public. Still, he noted that in the four years since the new state government was installed, one of the main goals of his team had been to "convert mezcal into a tourist product." This was the paradox of artisanal mezcal (indeed, of many artisanal products) and one that characterized Oaxaca itself: how to popularize and sell it while maintaining those very markers of authenticity, uniqueness, and quality cherished by its most adoring fans. The dilemma was not lost on the official, who was in charge of integrating mezcal into the strategic plan of a state whose economic revenue relied disproportionately on tourism. In fact, at the time of our meeting, his office was frantically preparing to launch its newly curated route Los Caminos del Mezcal. The mezcal route was one of several *rutas turísticas* (tourist routes) created by the state, including two others that focused on local products: the Ruta Mágica de las Artesanías (a "magical" handicraft route) and the Ruta del Café Sierra Sur, highlighting Oaxaca's southern coffee growing area (see Oaxaca Travel, n.d.). I too thought that mezcal's trajectory would be distinct from tequila's, but not because I shared his conviction that mezcal was of superior quality and authenticity.

We have seen how the distinct paths taken by tequila and mezcal reflect Mexico's historically uneven development. I return to the subject here because many of the same factors that pushed tequila along its path underlie the more "developed" tourism infrastructure that characterizes the Tequila region today. Befitting Tequila's history of modern, market-driven alcohol production and distribution, its tourism industry, too, has a more commercial tinge, bolstered by corporate infrastructure as well as national and international heritage branding. The town of Tequila, just fifty-six kilometers from the city of Guadalajara, holds the distinction of being a *pueblo mágico* (magical town), part of a federal program launched in 2001 by Mexico's Secretariat of Tourism (SECTUR) to promote towns thought to offer an exceptional experience by virtue of their natural beauty, cultural offerings, or historical relevance (see México Desconocido, n.d.). The town itself offers charming architecture and attractive shopping venues, but visits to Tequila invariably focus on its eponymous alcoholic spirit (Millán Vázquez de la Torre et al. 2014). In 2006, a 35,019-hectare site named the Agave Landscape and Ancient Industrial Facilities of Tequila was added to the UNESCO World Heritage list, which exists to draw "attention to the wealth and diversity of Earth's cultural and natural heritage" though sites and practices of "outstanding universal value" (cited in Di Giovine 2008, 139; see also UNESCO, n.d.).

Closer inspection of the UNESCO proclamation indicates that the phrase "ancient industrial facilities" refers to the two-thousand-year-old tradition of making cloth and fermented beverages from agave (the proclamation clarifies that tequila developed later, in the sixteenth century). Putting aside debates about whether agave distillation is an ancient Mesoamerican technology, we can observe that the site's attraction for modern-day tourists is that it fulfills a desire for what Marie Sarita Gaytán (2014, 91) calls "hacienda fantasy heritage." She argues that visitors come to Tequila not only to experience the agave spirit, but also to enact their romantic ideas about life on Mexican haciendas, the large, landed estates originating in Spanish colonial times. In the same vein that American film classic *Gone with the Wind* depicted bucolic scenes of southern plantation life—expansive cotton fields, Greek Revival homes, and landed gentry—the hacienda fantasy heritage offers tourists sweeping landscapes filled with row after row of neatly tended agave plants, Spanish colonial hacienda homes, and a docile, sanitized version of agricultural labor. Mexican telenovela fans may recognize this same fantasy as the backdrop of 2007's *Destilando Amor* (Distilling Love). This successful television series starred actress Angélica Rivera (wife of Enrique Peña Nieto, who would serve as president of Mexico in 2012–2018) as "La Gaviota" (the Seagull), a nickname she carries to this day. Rivera played a poor young woman who finds work as a *jimadora* (agave harvester) in the fields of Tequila, only to find romance and, ultimately, upward mobility in the form of a job on the Tequila Regulatory Council (CRT).

In the Tequila region, UNESCO heritage branding and conservation efforts have helped co-create a rural landscape where two of the largest tequila companies in the world, José Cuervo and Casa Herradura, have a significant presence. Visitors can take a train tour of the Tequila countryside and production process via the Tequila Express or José Cuervo Express, the latter of which, according to the company website, promises its riders that they will "feel like a traveler from another era . . . [with] all the glamour of yesteryear" (José Cuervo Express, n.d.). The glamour, one surmises, is associated with the hacienda owners and not the peons who worked the estates. Before COVID-19 hit in 2020, tours started at around ninety-five US dollars for a basic package and featured mariachi and *ballet folklórico* performances, onboard tequila tastings hosted by costumed attendants, and educational programming. They also included the opportunity to see *jimadores* who were ostensibly at work, but who sported unsoiled, matching outfits more suited to an episode of *Destilando Amor* than to the real physical demands of agricultural labor. During their stay in the *pueblo mágico* of Tequila, visitors can shuttle about in special buses shaped like tequila barrels and bottles and even chile peppers. Of course, not all visitors want that type of commercial experience, in which case there are providers offering tours to smaller production sites. Because tequila production runs the gamut from small, family producers to large, industrial facilities, one may find everything from packed, bottle-shaped tour buses and trains to customized visits to craft distilleries in more rustic settings.

It is easy to see Oaxacan mezcal as having the same tourism potential as tequila. Oaxaca is consistently singled out as a top world tourist destination for food and drink lovers, and tequila is, after all, a type of mezcal. Is it such a stretch to imagine a passenger train leisurely snaking through the Oaxacan countryside, allowing visitors to gaze at agave-filled landscapes while employees tend to them in regional ethnic attire? I casually mentioned the idea of Oaxaca turning into a "mini Tequila" to an acquaintance who worked in the same office as the official who had so vehemently denied a comparison between the two spirits. This acquaintance's sarcasm-laced response underscored how tourism in Mexico had fractured along class lines: "Please, we [the Secretariat of Tourism] want to attract people who like Lila Downs, not the *nacos* [uncultured/low-class] who listen to Los Bukis." The reference to Los Bukis—a Mexican *grupero* band that hit peak popularity in the 1980s, particularly among rural middle- and working-class Mexicans—drove home his point. The Secretariat of Tourism wanted to shape Oaxaca into a tourist destination that was more in line with Santa Fe, New Mexico, with its abundance of upscale restaurants and galleries featuring Native American artists, than with other, more "low-brow" destinations, like Branson, Missouri, with its theme park atmosphere, or the Florida Panhandle, colloquially derided as the "Redneck Riviera" (Jackson 2013). The tendency to view Tequila's accessibility and broad appeal as a negative smacked of elitism. Yet it aligned with a sentiment that I had increasingly encountered over the past twenty years, a belief that Oaxaca was becoming overexposed and too popular with tourists and expats.

It is tongue in cheek to say that Oaxaca is not in danger of being overrun by Los Bukis fans who also fancy themselves to be artisanal mezcal connoisseurs. But even with the apparent success of its arts-culture-food model, there are still major geographic and economic constraints to scaling up mezcal tourism to the level of tequila tourism in the state of Jalisco, where the National Chamber of the Tequila Industry estimated in 2018 that the industry was supporting nearly seventy thousand jobs and had generated 4.2 billion pesos (over US$5 million) over the course of a year in tax revenue alone (McClain 2018). Incorporating tequila tourism into a statewide development plan was not much of a stretch, with several key factors facilitating a symbiotic, interconnected regional touristic zone, particularly the density and size of tequila producers in a relatively compact geographic area, and the visually compelling agricultural landscape featuring expansive, uniformly planted agave fields (a sign of commercial monocropping that, sadly, has made the region vulnerable to negative environmental consequences as well as economic exploitation) (Valenzuela and Nabhan 2004). Other key factors include Tequila's UNESCO World Heritage designation, its proximity to Guadalajara and a major international airport, and the ease of travel to a long-established, accessible coastal resort industry anchored by Puerto Vallarta and a partial segment of Pacific coastline known as the "Costalegre." And while a 2014 study predicted that Tequila was ripe for developing into a food destination (Millán Vázquez de la Torre et al. 2014), tequila tourism did not depend on this development occurring. Tequila's brand recognition alone, inside and outside of Mexico, was enough.

In contrast with tequila, mezcal saw both its early commercialization and more recent efforts to promote mezcal-focused tourism hindered by certain endemic factors. For one, mezcal production takes place in zones scattered throughout the mountainous and geographically large state (Mexico's fifth largest), often in family-controlled operations in rural communities that are difficult to reach from the tourist hubs of Oaxaca City and beach towns like Puerto Escondido or Huatulco. The atomized nature of mezcal production is further exacerbated by a far-from-ideal transportation network, with issues ranging from perpetually unfinished road projects to frequent blockades (due to civil unrest) of the roads leading to the three-gate airport terminal in Oaxaca City. Prior to the downturn in tourism due to COVID-19, journalist Gustavo Arellano (2018) observed that not even the capital's booming restaurant scene was immune to the regular cycle of strikes and demonstrations, many of which are orchestrated by members of Section 22, the Oaxacan branch of Mexico's teachers union. Oaxaca's Pacific coastline boasts well-known beach destinations, but, until a new highway opened in spring 2024, these could only be reached by a five- to seven-hour trip along a curvy highway or an airplane flight from the capital. As for UNESCO World Heritage titles, Oaxaca holds two, one for Oaxaca City's colonial center and the other for Monte Albán, but neither focuses on mezcal or agave. And while there are a handful of larger, commercial facilities (e.g., Benevá and Casa Armando Guillermo Prieto) near Oaxaca City, they come nowhere close to the scale of the tequila manufacturing found in Jalisco—and if my visits, often with me as the only tourist, are any indication, they do not seem to attract many visitors. While tequila may now be experiencing a return to its artisanal roots, Oaxacan mezcal, for the most part, never moved beyond them in the first place.[2]

Mezcal is not and never will be tequila—and that includes how mezcal got to be and continues to evolve into an object of tourism. In the final sections of this chapter, I describe two approaches to creating a mezcal "experience," illustrating how the skilled tourist consumer shapes Oaxaca's mezcal tourism, making it, at least for now, a distinct and more specialized market than what is found in Tequila.

Los Caminos del Mezcal

I first heard about the plan to build a mezcal tourist route in 2013, when a friend mentioned that he had attended a meeting of mezcal producers from his hometown of Santiago Matatlán to discuss the merits of the proposed development. It turned out that not everyone in the "mezcal capital of the world," as the town billed itself, supported the plan. The route was to direct tourists along a forty-eight-kilometer stretch of the Pan-American Highway, connecting Oaxaca City to Matatlán and encompassing towns and sights in between. The plan also called for the construction of a factory to produce agave syrup, a popular sweetener vying to become a sugar alternative. Objections to the tentatively named

"Ruta del Mezcal" were wide ranging. A common concern was that only businesses located directly on the road would be visible to tourists, most of whom would be driving by car, taxi, or tourist van. Among those who were lucky to occupy prime highway real estate, there were worries about having to remodel their buildings to comply with design standards meant to create a more uniform appearance along the road, which also served as Matatlán's main thoroughfare. One resident even noted the construction's potential to disrupt at the microbial level the delicate airborne yeasts that flourished in individual *palenques* and contributed to the unique flavor profiles of their mezcals. Still others lamented that the route was hardly representative of mezcal production in Oaxaca, as most stops along the way were known for other things, such as handicrafts or the giant Tule tree, a much-visited two-thousand-year-old Montezuma cypress, among the oldest and widest trees in the world. While there may have been logistical reasons for choosing Matatlán as the route's anchor point, mezcal producers said that they felt left out by the decision. Among those who expressed this opinion were producers from Santa Catarina Minas, famous for its mezcal distilled in clay pots.

More than anything, though, I sensed apathy from local residents. Government corruption and a history of shoddily constructed and incomplete projects bred skepticism. Indeed, few were surprised when, in 2014, the Mexican newspaper *Milenio* ran an article declaring that the Ruta del Mezcal was "in limbo" due to the lack of a strategic marketing plan. The article quoted José Zorrilla, Oaxaca's secretary of tourism at the time, who defended the stalled project. He promised "not just to launch a tourist product, a slogan or a brand. . . . This year we are going to promote the Ruta del Mezcal, which will be better than tequila's, but not until we have completed a strategic plan, which includes infrastructure (bridges and highways), hotels, walkways, services, and restaurants. This will benefit all of the mezcal-producing zones of the state and will be financed by the federal government" (quoted in Rodríguez 2014). The plan eventually came to fruition—sort of. Early in 2015, signs marking the route began to appear along the highway to Matatlán. The route was now rebranded as Los Caminos del Mezcal because the name Ruta del Mezcal had already been trademarked by a group of private businesses in Oaxaca City. Matatlán received funding to widen the main stretch of highway into a tourist "boulevard," which also entailed the construction of covered taxi stops and structural improvements to some buildings. However, since it is a federal highway, creating the sort of quaint byway that tourists might have found attractive—paved with cobblestones and

Figure 4.2 Sign announcing the project for the "Betterment of Santiago Matatlán's Urban Image" at the 2015 inauguration of Los Caminos del Mezcal. Photo by author.

featuring shaded, pedestrian-friendly sidewalks—proved logistically complicated. As for the new bridges, hotels, and other services, they had not yet materialized.

In March 2015 I attended the inauguration of Los Caminos del Mezcal in Matatlán. Zorrilla, members of the organizing committee, and the Oaxaca state governor, Gabino Cué Monteagudo, were in attendance. Amid much pomp and circumstance, residents from Matatlán and surrounding communities gathered under a giant tent, where they listened to presentations describing the success of the plan, which the government had named the "Betterment of Santiago Matatlán's Urban Image" (see figure 4.2). In the background, two giant screens projected before and after shots of the improvements, along with images of other tourist attractions around the state, among them Puerto Escondido with its surfing culture and the annual Guelaguetza festival in Oaxaca City. The takeaway was that mezcal tourism was poised to join the menu of other already-popular leisure activities. I was sitting between my friend from Matatlán and two women from San Juan Guelavía, an Indigenous Zapotec town just a short drive off the main highway and the mezcal route. It was also a well-established center for basketry woven from a bamboo-like river reed known as *carrizo*; like numerous Oaxacan crafts, this basketry now had its own yearly festival. I asked the women whether they were enthused about the potential for increased tourism to their community as a result of the new route, but the suggestion did not seem to resonate with either of them. One said that they had come because they heard there was going to be live music and free ice cream. From my other side, my friend chimed in to say that the inauguration was a "farce," a show to prove that the government was working for the people, and that even if the improvements looked nice they were not going to dramatically increase tourist traffic.

For all his pessimism, my friend appeared to be right. Despite the cosmetic changes that came with the route branding, the sort of car traffic that might have transformed Matatlán into a bustling tourist hub never materialized. On my subsequent visits to the town over the next three years, the owners of shops and *palenques* along the main thoroughfare reported little uptick in business, and outside of spots along this main strip selling mezcal and inexpensive souvenirs, Matatlán still had little in the way of tourist services. Visitors who did come to check out mezcal typically came with a guide who took them directly to a specific producer or *palenque* and spent very little time in other parts of the community. So why was Los Caminos del Mezcal not more successful at generating tourism? It is easy to write off the route as just another in a long line of ill-conceived or poorly executed state infrastructure projects. Admittedly, the finished project fell short of the more grandiose vision originally proposed. But more than that, state planners had failed to consider those providers and consumers who had paved the way for mezcal tourism and who continued to exert the most influence over the market; by its very design, a self-guided highway route did not align with the interests of this self-selecting group of tourists.

Mezcal on Tour

"It took gringos falling in love with mezcal for Mexicans to begin to take notice of the stuff." In 2015 I attended a two-day event in Oaxaca City organized by pioneering figures of the local mezcal scene.[3] In between expert talks on agave biodiversity and the biochemical processes involved in tasting mezcal, I chatted with an American entrepreneur who was visiting Oaxaca with the goal of starting his own export brand. Though somewhat off-putting—and reductive, since it ignored the long history of local Oaxacan mezcal consumption and a craft mezcal renaissance in Mexico City—his remark echoed Jeffrey Pilcher's (2010) reminder that we cannot overlook the outsize role played by Mexico's historical relationship with and proximity to the United States in shaping perceptions of Mexican places, products, and people. It also echoed a lament that I had heard from non-Mexicans and Mexicans alike: that artisanal mezcal had to first gain traction with Americans for Mexicans of a certain social status to see its value.

The same may be said of mezcal tourism. While this industry has not been exclusively dominated by "gringos," Americans and Canadians (including expats living in Mexico) have played an outsize role in its development. Domingo García Garza (2021) characterizes the evolution of mezcal tourism as comprising three stages. He notes that some of the earliest mezcal tourists were, in fact, local politicians, artists, and, importantly, chefs, who were among the first to draw attention to the drink as part the boom around 2010. An important figure in this first wave was Ron Cooper, the founder of Del Maguey Mezcal. Cooper is famously credited with importing the first artisanal mezcal to the United States in the 1990s, but his role in facilitating early mezcal tourism was equally important. He brought scores of bar and culinary professionals to Oaxaca to see the production of mezcal (and his brand) firsthand (Cooper and Martineau 2018).

A transition period (or second wave) between 2014 and 2015 saw the rise of microdistillery tours primarily designed by Americans and Canadians, most of whom owned or worked with specific brands, bars, or other sectors of the hospitality industry. Such tours were mainly aimed at English-speaking tourists from North America, but they also opened the door for a third wave of tourists, this time from Europe, Australia, Asia, and South America (García Garza 2021, 69). Notably absent from García Garza's timeline are the middle-class Mexicans who account for a significant segment of Oaxaca's tourists. Even today (although this is changing with the overall growth of the industry, particularly as more and more Mexicans begin to lead excursions), mezcal draws few visitors from the wide swath of Mexican tourists who visit Oaxaca each year. Middle-class Mexicans may demonstrate the economic means to consume mezcal as tourists or otherwise, but an appreciation of artisanal mezcal has not yet become ingrained as part of the cultural capital associated with middle-class status in the way it has in the United States.[4]

My fieldwork fortuitously spanned the years between 2011 and

2018, allowing me to observe the evolution of mezcal tourism almost from its inception by participating in excursions led by some of its earliest innovators, two Americans and one Canadian, all men, who permanently resided in Oaxaca.[5] While these tour leaders do not necessarily represent the full spectrum of mezcal tourism found in Oaxaca today, they established a model that is still emulated by others in the industry. Notably, what these tours had in common were their scale and setting, with visits taking place in small distilleries located in rural or semirural communities outside of Oaxaca City, many in Indigenous, Zapotec-speaking villages. Most of these distilleries produced commercial brands, among them, Real Minero in Santa Catarina Minas, Del Maguey Vida in San Luis del Río, Wahaka Mezcal in San Dionisio Ocotepec, and Tosba Mezcal in San Cristóbal Lachirioag.

In contrast to tequila tourism, with its underlying hacienda fantasy heritage (Gaytán 2014), mezcal tourism is not about evoking the opulence of Mexico's bygone agricultural estates—quite the opposite. García Garza (2021) argues that fantasy heritage still drives the tourist experience, but instead of hacienda life it is based on life on ranchos, which are clustered in small settlements or villages where campesinos farm and raise livestock. Indeed, the places we visited often projected an aura of rusticity associated with Mexican country life (see Stanford 2012). Regardless of whether an Indigenous language was being spoken, there was an underlying assumption that these were Indigenous communities.[6] It was not uncommon to visit distilleries in household compounds where extended family members were cooking meals, washing laundry, feeding animals, or preparing harvested corn for storage. Such images of rural rusticity were mirrored, in turn, in the lack of modernization of the *palenques* themselves, whose more traditional production methods afforded visitors with experiences not available in the industrial distilleries more characteristic of the Tequila region. For instance, we were personally introduced to the *maestro mezcalero* (master mezcal maker) as we learned about the unique details of each facility, such as spring water carried down a steep hill in an impossibly long rubber hose and an innovative steam oven jerry-rigged by a producer with an engineering background. At one *palenque*, we watched two young men use heavy wooden *mazos* (mallets) to hand-grind fresh agave hearts in a hulled-out wooden vessel known in Spanish as a *canoa*. In another, we listened intently as our guide demonstrated how to measure alcohol volume the traditional way, using a simple tube made from *carrizo*. At yet another facility, the able-bodied tourists among us took turns splitting agave hearts with axes and loading

Figure 4.3 Visitors to a *palenque* try their hand at crushing roasted agave using traditional wooden mallets. Photo by author.

them into a wood-fired pit oven for roasting (see figure 4.3). At a mezcal "boot camp" held at the Tosba distillery in San Cristóbal Lachirioag, we circled around the producer as he gave a culinary demonstration of how he preps the ingredients for *mezcal de pechuga,* a mezcal that traditionally contains a chicken or turkey breast along with special blends of fruits and spices. Later that evening, the same producer prepared for our group a feast that included grilled *tejón* (coatimundi). He explained to me that he had proposed homemade ravioli, a recipe he had picked up working in an Italian restaurant in California, but that his conversation with the tour leader convinced him that the group would prefer food that was locally sourced and "culturally appropriate."

These visits were meant to feel organic rather than staged, even as they were highly routinized and performative. Scholars since Dean MacCannell ([1976] 1999) have emphasized that a primary driver of tourism is the "search for authenticity," a quality that is perceived to be lacking in modern life, and growing more so under late capitalism. Mezcal tourism certainly promises an authentic experience—some would say one that is more authentic than the so-called staged tourism found in Tequila. But debating whether one place is more "real" than the other is a self-defeating exercise. All tourism—and the people it mobilizes as tourists and "locals"—actively shapes the way that places are toured and their continued evolution as a result.

In the case of mezcal, the tourists it has attracted from the beginning have overwhelmingly demonstrated markers of connoisseurship, including, but not limited to, an understanding of terroir and the finer points of distillation and fermentation processes as applied to a wide range of alcoholic drinks. The tourist client base has undoubtedly expanded in recent years, but as of 2018 industry professionals—restaurateurs, mixologists, chefs, brewers, distillers, and sommeliers—still outnumbered even the adventurous foodies I met on tours. These professionals were at the forefront of the artisanal food and beverage renaissance in the United States, among them a man who had traveled to Japan to study the craft of sake making; a married couple that had just opened a microdistillery in Utah; the owner of a craft brewery in Philadelphia, Pennsylvania; and the founder of Tales of the Cocktail, one of the biggest annual conferences for cocktail and spirits professionals and enthusiasts in the United States. In some cases, visitors to mezcal distilleries blurred the lines between tourism and entrepreneurship, such as the restauranteur from Seattle, Washington, who was putting together a mezcal menu for his newly opened café serving Oaxacan cuisine, or the multiple individuals who expressed interest in founding their own mezcal brands or import companies.

The very specific nature of mezcal tourism is not just happenstance. Here it is instructive to consider mezcal among what Didier Chabrol and José Muchnik (2011) term "heritage food products." These are a special category of comestibles whose continuation and diffusion depend on the "'consumption skills and technologies' . . . the set of knowledge, know-how and techniques used by 'non-producer actors' of the supply chain and especially consumers, to obtain the expected utility or service from a food product." Critically, the authors contend that the success of a heritage food relies just as much on the skilled consumer as on the producer, the place, or even the very qualities of the product itself; there is no market for a heritage food or drink without the consumer. A similar logic applies when the production site of a heritage food product becomes an object of tourism and a market emerges around it. A tension arises when it is taken for granted that the place can shape its own economic destiny without those skilled consumers. This is one of the main reasons why the middle-class Mexicans who have made up the largest segment of Oaxaca tourists are still underrepresented on mezcal tours.

For many of them, mezcal is still a drink of the rural poor, not a product that is representative of a collective national heritage in the same way that tequila is (Gaytán 2018), although this perception is rapidly changing. It is also why the highway tourism envisioned by the government never took off; the profile of the tourists it was most likely to attract—arguably less discerning highway travelers—did not necessarily overlap with those most interested in mezcal, whose substantial food and drink expertise demanded something other than a street lined with shops selling largely undifferentiated products and offering little opportunity for hands-on engagement with producers and the production process.

Mezcal tourism is not "behind" tequila tourism; it is embedded in the wider tourism market of Oaxaca, which is in the process of reimagining and rebranding popular and folk culture to become one of the premiere food and art destinations in the country, if not the world. Moreover, we should not assume that there was simply a place (Oaxaca) and a product (mezcal), and then people started to show up. Such a view ignores the more complicated dynamic by which a place like Oaxaca becomes a centrifuge for the skilled tourist consumer. These movements have created a set of people who view themselves as both consumer and expert, insider and outsider. They were enlisted to "experience Oaxaca" and inadvertently created the brand they wanted to cultivate. Tourism is not the final outcome—as most people assume—but rather an invitation to continue building the Oaxaca brand, one where mole and mezcal are prepared under unadulterated ancient skies, and, as of October 2022, tourists can stay in Lila Downs's newly listed Airbnb.

5 | Valuing Women or Creating Value?

"You don't know Reyna?" asked Ulises Torrentera, his eyebrows raised in disbelief. Torrentera was the author of several books on mezcal and one of Oaxaca's foremost experts on the subject (Torrentera 2001, 2009, 2017). More recently he had opened a small mezcal tasting bar, In Situ, in downtown Oaxaca City with partner Sandra Ortíz Brena. Between the two of them there was hardly a producer or type of mezcal that went uncataloged, and their tiny space quickly gained fame for showcasing the best artisanal mezcal in the city. "You have to meet her, she's badass [*bien chingona*]," continued Torrentera. His glowing endorsement had come in response to a question from me about whether he knew of any *mezcaleras,* or female mezcal makers, in Oaxaca. Up until that point, I had met countless women in *mezcalero* households and *palenques* (mezcal distilleries). Yet most did not self-identify as mezcal producers, a role typically ascribed to a male member of the extended household, be it a husband, son, brother, or father.

Torrentera's endorsement convinced me that I should seek out Reyna Sánchez, whose first name (often interchangeably spelled "Reina") was the Spanish word for "queen," serendipitously evoking royalty. "The queen of mezcal," I thought. I soon learned that this association was not far from reality. It turned out that Sánchez was something of a phenomenon in the mezcal world. In fact, she was one of a handful of Oaxacan women who, at the time, had become synonymous with the term *maestra mezcalera* itself; the fact that she was recognized by name was emblematic of the gender exceptionalism that pervaded the mezcal world. It dawned on me that I had, in fact, previously encountered her—

or at least a photo of her. It was on a bottle of mezcal that I saw displayed behind the counter at Cuish, a hole-in-the-wall bar near Oaxaca's red-light district. Owned by local artist and entrepreneur Félix Hernández Monterrosa, whose parents once ran an *expedio de mezcal* (small mezcal shop) in the same location, Cuish was among the first of the new breed of *mezcalerías* to take off in the city after its founding in 2009. In the photo on the bottle, Sánchez was wearing the typical uniform of many Oaxacan women, a colorful, embroidered *mandil* (apron), along with an atypical black cowboy hat, and holding a bottle of mezcal in her outstretched hands. I set out to understand not only how she came to be such a local celebrity, but also why she, and not the many other women involved in mezcal production, had captured the public imagination.

Sánchez was forty-nine years old when I first met her in person in 2015, and she lived in the same rural community where she was born. Lachigüizo, with its population of around one hundred people, was more of a hamlet than a town. But in recent years, it, along with other communities from the municipality of San Luis Amatlán in Miahuatlán District, had developed a reputation for producing some of the finest artisanal mezcals on the market. It had now started to garner attention from outsiders, who had previously shown little interest in this largely untouristed corner of Oaxaca, which boasted neither a beach nor the folkloric cultural attractions and lifestyle amenities of the state capital.

Sánchez learned the tasks associated with agricultural life and mezcal-making from a young age. Her father was in the military and frequently absent, leaving her in the care of her grandparents and mother. By her own account, her grandfather Ignacio Sánchez played an especially important role in her upbringing, teaching her from a young age to care for the family's livestock and assigning her small tasks as he seasonally distilled mezcal in the family's rustic *palenque*. She found she enjoyed this work as much as if not more than the household chores that young girls in her community were expected to perform. Thus, in addition to the usual domestic skill set acquired by rural women, such as childcare and food preparation, she also developed under her grandfather's tutelage an aptitude for mezcal-making.

More than forty years later, her grandfather long deceased, Sánchez still lived with her elderly, nearly blind mother, just the two of them, in a house that until recently had sported an earthen floor. Thanks to a government loan she was finally able to pour a concrete floor for her house, as well as for the rustic *palenque* that sat adjacent. The first time I visited her there, I noticed a shiny, full-size pickup truck parked squarely in front of her house. When I asked her about it, she described with great pride that was also tinged with profound sadness how it had been a gift from her two adult children, a daughter and a son, who years before had left to work in the United States and had not returned since. Unfortunately, like many Oaxacan women of her generation from rural communities, she never learned how to drive, depending instead on *colectivos* (communal taxis) and buses for transportation. The young men she hired to help in the *palenque* occasionally used the truck to haul materials, but most days it served for hanging a clothesline for drying laundry.

I would go back to Sánchez's house at least a half dozen more times during my fieldwork, visits not easily arranged since she had virtually no cell phone reception near her house and there was no other way to contact her. Midmorning on Mondays was the best time to call her, she let me know, because she traveled to Miahuatlán's weekly market, about thirty minutes away by *colectivo*, to do her shopping. There was no shortage of people who wanted to meet her, and a number of them accompanied me to her home on different occasions; this included a Mexican photographer, a Polish anthropologist, an American journalist, and the founders of both Mezcalistas (an online mezcal resource) and Experience Agave (a tequila/mezcal tour business). Sánchez was also a member of Maestros del Mezcal, a civil association whose aim was to promote small producers. This took her away from home as she traveled to meetings and events with the group, often in Oaxaca City but sometimes farther away.

Every visit with Sánchez was a special occasion, or at least it felt like one. In Lachigüizo she warmly welcomed me and any other guests with delicious food prepared in her outdoor kitchen, copious amounts of mezcal, and guided tours of her *palenque* and the surrounding area, where she both cultivated and collected agave. I quickly learned to wear long pants and sturdy shoes, since visits often included lengthy impromptu treks that followed no discernible road to visit neighbors or to scout for wild agaves on nearby land that had yet to be cleared of its thick vegetation.

On one particularly joyful occasion, I arrived at Sánchez's home just in time to join a crew that was there to survey some nearby land that she had recently acquired. Guided by a local official who went by the nickname of "El Escorpión" (the Scorpion) and had a tattoo to prove it, we ran what felt like the world's longest ball of twine up and down hills around the property's sizable perimeter, cutting through dense brush with machetes, in order to measure and temporarily mark its boundaries. After we returned to her house, Sánchez and her mother set to work making tortillas and dishing up the mole she had ground herself the day before in the ancient mill that stood next to the concrete slab where she cooked on a hearth over an open fire. As usual, Sánchez bustled about in one of her signature color-coordinated blouse and skirt sets, paired with matching earrings and nail polish from one of the dozens of bottles she kept neatly lined up against a wall in her bedroom. She wore a wide-brimmed hat, which I came to realize was not only a matter of sun protection but also part of a unique fashion sensibility that had become her trademark. A party ensued, as neighbors continued to drop by throughout the day to offer their congratulations and share in the food and drink.

Needless to say, the perceived rarity of a *maestra mezcalera* generated numerous requests for appearances and interviews. On more than one occasion, I watched Sánchez patiently recount to an inquiring visitor how she had come to make mezcal. Sometimes her personal story stood alone, but more often it was combined with those of other women involved in mezcal production; examples include a 2015 story that aired on the public radio program the *World*, where she was identified as one of "three women blazing a trail in the red-hot mezcal industry" (Rubenstein 2015), and "Maestras Mezcaleras," a special event hosted by La Olla, a popular Oaxaca City restaurant, featuring a Q and A with Sánchez and fellow rising *mezcalera* Berta Vásquez, a Zapotec woman from San Baltazar Chichicapam (see figure 5.1). Tourists, too, began to seek out Sánchez. Alvin Starkman, a Canadian lawyer who retired in Oaxaca and has become a successful mezcal tour leader, remarked to me in one of our many conversations that he had increasingly received special requests from clients to visit Sánchez at her home in Lachigüizo (pers. comm. 2015).

One might view all this interest and publicity as a positive outcome for Sánchez. Indeed, it established her presence in the craft mezcal world, generating a somewhat steady demand for her product. But apart from sales at special events hosted by Maestros del Mezcal or made to the occasional tourist, most of her income came from selling *a granel* (in bulk) to Mezcalería Cuish, where I had first seen her photo. One late afternoon as we drove in my car to Oaxaca City to deliver a last-minute mezcal order, she expressed her frustration at having to sell her product wholesale through a middleman. "Everyone tells me how good my mezcal is, well, you've tried it! I know that it's worth more, but I don't have any other option." I sympathized with her situation. It was one that small-scale craft producers, male and female alike, faced when wanting to sell their mezcal outside of traditional markets—that is, beyond their direct community or regional networks. In Sánchez's case, she did not

Figure 5.1 Reyna Sánchez (*left*) and Berta Vásquez pose beside bottles bearing their photos at the "Maestras Mezcaleras" event in Oaxaca City, 2015. Photo by author.

have the resources to bottle, brand, and distribute her own mezcal even in Oaxaca City, let alone to the national or international market. Sánchez told me that a few brand owners and exporters had approached her about buying and rebranding her product under their own label, but at the time nothing had panned out.

That aside, many of the challenges that Sánchez faced stemmed from the fact that she was a woman. More critically, she was a rural woman who had never married, a fact she was frank about when recounting her story. Her children in the United States helped out to the extent they were able, but they had their own families. With neither a husband nor children nearby to support her, Sánchez had little choice but to find work that could supplement her household's meager subsistence production, which consisted of maintaining a small milpa (garden plot) and raising a few animals. Some other women in the community wove baskets and other small crafts out of palm fibers, a technique that Sánchez had also learned but whose potential for generating income was minimal in comparison with mezcal.

Reflecting on Sánchez's situation, I recalled a female friend in Oaxaca once telling me that one of the best times in a rural Oaxacan woman's life was widowhood. At first I was confused at this, because that status implied the loss of a husband. Yet I later realized what she meant. Widowhood represented a stage in life when most women have complied with the social expectations of marriage and childbearing, granting them full adult status in their communities; and also a time when they are no longer subject to the demands of their male spouses, granting them a sort of freedom previously unavailable. This was not a judgment of Oaxacan men per se, but more a commentary on the prescribed gender roles that still governed life in rural villages (and arguably also in urban areas), in which the typical female trajectory included marriage and children, not a professional path (see Howell 2023).

As a single mother, Sánchez did not conform to this social ideal, and the fact that she followed the traditionally male vocational path of becoming a *mezcalera* made her even more of an anomaly among her peers.[1] This granted her a considerable amount of freedom for a woman. For instance, there was no one to dictate her movements, allowing her to make semifrequent trips to Oaxaca City and to travel with others from Maestros del Mezcal, whose members were disproportionately male. Likewise, she was free to interact as she liked, joking or taking a shot of mezcal, with friends or new acquaintances. It was no coincidence that Sánchez was frequently described as a "spitfire," someone "rowdy," "feisty," "fun," and "badass." These characteristics were undoubtedly an intrinsic part of Sánchez's personality, but her sidestepping of local gender conventions allowed them the space to more openly flourish. In this way she mirrored the women from Oaxaca's Isthmus of Tehuantepec. *Tehuanas* have long been celebrated in Mexico not only for their beautiful regional clothing but as symbols of female empowerment, the latter attributed to their direct control over market activities and other economic resources (Chassen-López 2014).

Yet the success or freedom apparently enjoyed by unmarried woman like Sánchez can often function as a double-edged sword in their rural communities. The very behaviors that some take as markers of female empowerment—working, socializing, or traveling outside of community boundaries, literal or figurative—can make women the target of criticism or speculation. When I spoke with Félix Hernández Monterrosa, the owner of Mezcalería Cuish, I asked him what he thought of Sánchez's growing reputation as a *maestra mezcalera*. He replied that it was hard won, adding that there were some who refused to believe that women could make high-quality mezcal by themselves, claiming that there must be someone else (a man) behind the spirit's production. Yet he stood by his female producers, not just Sánchez but also Berta Vásquez, who had turned to mezcal as a means to support her household after she lost both her husband and her elder son. "It hasn't been at all easy for Reyna,"

Monterrosa said. It seemed that her newfound celebrity had not translated to respect or status in Lachigüizo. If anything, he said, it had caused her to become more of an outsider, as her work took her further afield from the roles occupied by her female peers. Nevertheless, Sánchez persevered—it was not in her nature to stop doing the work she liked and did well, nor could she afford to do so.

Monterrosa eventually, in 2019, branded and certified many of the mezcals he sold under the Cuish label, including ones produced by Sánchez, and began exporting outside them outside of Mexico.[2] This has further increased Sánchez's visibility as a *maestra mezcalera,* even though, as of 2024, she has not established her own brand. It has also contributed to the growing recognition that women, in fact, do make mezcal, including a newer generation of women who are intentionally choosing this path. The number of Oaxacan women who fall into this category will undoubtedly continue to grow in years to come. Of course, there are countless women in the mezcal industry who themselves are not considered to be producers like Reyna Sánchez. Subsequent sections of this chapter describe the various roles women play, whether it be brand owner, influencer, or invisible wage or household laborer. What all these examples have in common is that they illustrate how the celebration of women in mezcal tends to elide the difficult social and material realities they face in entering and participating in this male-dominated industry.

Locating Women in Mezcal

> This mezcal is balls to the wall. It's powerful with a luxurious sweetness at its foundation. For me it is best enjoyed neat. The fruity vanilla body coats your whole mouth and the finish is smooth. The alcohol does some subtle pummeling to your tongue, but it is most pleasurable. I highly recommend torching up a killer cigar and pouring a double of this. Crank up your favorite music and sit back and enjoy. Your senses will become aroused. Enjoy it with your lady friend. And if she doesn't like it she should not be your lady friend.
>
> Review of Del Maguey Chichicapa, Mezcal Reviews

As with many semi-anonymous mezcal reviews found online, one might deduce the above author's gender identity. While I have no way of proving it, clues such as the reviewer's username (MitchVortex), profile tag line ("Mezcal. Cigars. Chicks. Life."), and phallocentric enthusiasm for mezcal suggest maleness—or at least a particular version of it (Mezcal Reviews, n.d.a.). For many US English speakers, this linguistic register or speaking style is associated with a particular form of hegemonic masculinity that has come to be known in the North American lexicon as "bro culture" (Lawson 2020). Writing about the evolution of the term *bro* for *New York Magazine*, journalist Ann Friedman (2013) notes that "bro once meant something specific: a self-absorbed young white guy in board shorts with a taste for cheap beer. But it's become a shorthand for the sort of privileged ignorance that thrives in groups dominated by wealthy, white, straight men."

Stereotypes of men and women in relationship to alcohol abound, from the indisputably masculine connotations of whiskey to so-called girly drinks like daiquiris and cosmopolitans, the latter of which was popularized by the female-centric television series *Sex and the City* in the late 1990s. More recently, in 2020, Bacardi introduced its Plume & Petal line, which Kara Newman (2020), the spirits editor for *Wine Enthusiast*, sardonically described as a "'spa-inspired' lineup of low-calorie, low-alcohol vodkas aimed at 'the modern woman.'" Indeed, Barcardi received such harsh criticism in the press and on social media for its use of gendered language and stereotypical portrayals of female consumers that the company later issued a statement saying it was "not proud" of its choice in marketing strategy, even though the products purportedly had been made "by women, for women" (Carruthers 2020).

Mezcal has yet to be subjected to such easy-to-spot gendered marketing, though it may be on the way. In 2015, one Oaxacan mezcal brand owner told me that he was contemplating making a pink-tinged mezcal "because women gravitated to that color," and several pink mezcals—at least one colored by the natural insect dye cochineal—have in fact entered the market since then. At the same time, a bro culture of "wealthy, white, straight men" is alive and well in the mezcal world and has significant overlap with the skilled consumers driving mezcal tourism. It is a demographic whose disproportionately high economic and social capital cannot help but dictate the market, even though it in no way encompasses all those who drink mezcal. The mezcal market thus reinforces a binary system by which gender is expressed as two distinct, oppositional forms of masculine and feminine.

On the production side, as with craft brewing and winemaking, the distillation of hard alcohol also tends to be naturalized as men's work, even though women actively participate in all these industries. It is not that women are less capable brewers or winemakers; it is that so often they are not permitted to enter and publicly excel within those spheres of activity. Writing about folk art, another important Mexican craft industry, feminist scholar Eli Bartra (2011, 3) argues that the making of handicrafts may be understood only when "attention is paid to social division of genders, in other words the hierarchical division between men and women." The same is true for mezcal. Nearly all the women I spoke with during my years of mezcal research mentioned the challenges and frustrations of working in a male-dominated spirits world, describing varying degrees of sexism that occasionally veered toward harassment. Their lived experiences of gender inequality within the industry, for the most part, went unaddressed even as women's overall visibility increased. With the exception of the few hardscrabble individuals, like Reyna Sánchez, who have made names for themselves as *maestras mezcaleras*, much women's work goes unacknowledged, giving the impression, perhaps, of novelty rather than the norm. One of the few publications by and about women in the mezcal industry affirms that "much of the work that we women do is, in some way or another, silent, but without it, families would not get ahead, we are talking about work that supports familial structure and cohesion" (Pardo Nuñez and Ángeles Carreño 2021, 6, my translation). As Graciela Ángeles Carreño, the driving force behind her family's successful Real Minero brand and one of the book's contributors, told me in an interview, "Women have always been involved in mezcal. It's just a question of whether people want to acknowledge it or not" (see figure 5.2).

To Ángeles Carreño's point, mezcal is so heavily gendered that when women participate in public roles, whether as makers or as entrepreneurs, it is still regarded as exceptional. Thus, the "discovery" and celebration of women in the mezcal industry often erases the very gender discrimination and inequities that created the circumstances by which women came to participate in the first place. I found that the exclusionary nature of mezcal production was often explained away as stemming from the physically demanding nature of the work itself. But this argument does not hold up well when one considers the other types of physically demanding labor that rural Mexican women frequently perform, such as tending agricultural fields and carrying heavy loads, which may include everything from firewood to young children.

Of course women make mezcal—they distill, bottle, transport, brand, and sell it. In this regard, this chapter puts to rest the basic assumption that women generally do not "make mezcal," which itself is a more complicated matter than the phrase implies. But more than that,

Figure 5.2 Graciela Ángeles Carreño of Real Minero discusses different types of agave used for mezcal. Photo by author.

this chapter considers the interwoven forces underlying the perception of mezcal as men's work. It reveals a market that depends on female invisibility to constantly reproduce an ideology of novelty and scarcity. This in turn is the foundation for an emerging market predicated on creating value through women's development and empowerment.

The Invisible Labor of Craft

"¡Ten cuidado, te va a caer la matriz!" (Be careful, your womb is going to fall!) the older woman shouted, evidently concerned that my strenuous efforts would lead to a prolapsed uterus, a serious medical condition that could potentially result in infertility. From where I stood in the back of the rickety truck, surrounded by tons of freshly cut agave hearts, my womb collapsing was the furthest thing from my mind. I considered myself healthy and youngish at thirty-nine years old and did not see any issue with helping the crew unload the plants. Transported that morning from a nearby field, the freshly cut agave hearts weighed in at over two hundred pounds each in some cases. I yelled back across the courtyard unloading area that I would be careful to not lift anything too heavy. The woman relented, shrugging her shoulders as if to say, "I warned you," and went back inside the house. Still, her comment gave me pause.

A handful of women from a nearby village worked part-time at the *palenque* owned by this woman's son. Yet I never saw them loading or unloading trucks or the giant in-ground pit where the agave was roasted. Likewise, they were mostly excluded from the distillation process. Their jobs were mainly limited to bottling and packing the finished product, which included, in this case, dipping the mouth of each bottle in hot wax and letting it drip down the neck to artful effect. As time went on, I visited a range of mezcal production sites, from simple stills in people's backyards to commercial facilities. I began to notice women's contributions, even when they were not immediately associated with the production process. Not only did I witness women undertaking some of the same physically demanding tasks as their male counterparts, I also saw them feed work crews, track production-related expenses, check the alcohol by volume (ABV) of newly distilled batches, and facilitate transactions with clients wanting to purchase mezcal. At Benevá, one of Oaxaca's largest commercial mezcal distilleries, located just outside of the city, not only were women on the bottling assembly line (see figure 5.3), but a female employee supervised the *área de gusanos* (worm area), a controlled-access room where countless thousands of maguey worms sat in sterile buckets of alcohol until their time came to be bottled.

Before I go any further, an admission: I did not start this research with an eye toward gender analysis. This means that I overlooked the fundamental question of who actually makes mezcal—or, at least, whose labor counts when we think about mezcal's value as a craft product. I had always assumed that male labor was the backbone of mezcal production,

Figure 5.3 A female worker at Benevá inspects a bottle of Monte Alban mezcal on the assembly line. Photo by author.

which was borne out by my initial observations working in the distillery. From the backbreaking work of harvesting agave plants with rudimentary, nonmechanized tools to that of tending hot, fire-fed stills, making mezcal could easily appear to be men's work. Yet women were almost always present, playing ancillary roles if not identified as primary makers themselves.

This should not have been surprising to me, given my previous experience living and doing research in a Oaxacan wood-carving community (see Brulotte 2012); there I had observed a gendered division of labor in household craft production that was not entirely unlike that of mezcal. Early in my fieldwork, I was eager to learn all aspects of the craft, despite the fact that I had never seen another woman carving. I tried, rather unsuccessfully, to carve a wooden giraffe under the watchful eye of my future compadre, himself a skilled artisan. Never having used a machete to sculpt, I was ultimately too terrified of cutting myself to finish it. Yet neither of us believed that carving was inherently gendered work, "too dangerous" for a woman, as some had told me. Rather, we both agreed that the skill involved years of training and practice, a path not typically an option for women in the community, who were socialized from an early age to assume other forms of labor in the household. The same may be said of mezcal.

Writing about the Oaxacan mezcal boom, Granville E. Greene (2017) places the spirit alongside other regional crafts, describing it as "edible folk art." And while there are many comparisons to be made with Oaxaca's *artesanías* (handicrafts), Green's analogy is especially helpful for thinking about how much of the labor of craft, whether making wood carvings or mezcal, goes unrecognized, and particularly how that reflects existing gender divisions. Given all the steps required to transform raw materials into a finished product, Oaxacan crafts often reflect the efforts of multiple people within and sometimes across households, rather than the person whose name appears on a piece or who is otherwise credited as the maker.

The popular wood carvings, for instance, typically bear the name of a single male artisan, usually the person responsible for carving (Chibnik 2003). Yet in addition to finely sanding carved figurines, women are often the ones behind the elaborate, painted designs that give Oaxacan wood carvings their signature look. Other local crafts rely also on social networks of varying complexity for their production, such as the Indigenous Zapotec weavings from the towns of Teotitlán del Valle and neighboring Santa Ana del Valle (see Cohen 1999; Stephen 2005; Wood 2008). The tasks of carding and dyeing wool and weaving the finished rug might be carried out by a specific individual, but more often this labor is divided among several people, both men and women. And this is to say nothing of marketing, where women are key actors (Stephen 2005). In contrast, other craft work, like embroidering textiles or making ceramics, is often regarded as the province of women, even when men actively participate (Wasserspring 2000). Enter the home workshop of Oaxacan ceramicist Josefina Aguilar, known for her playful clay figurines, and one is likely to see the entire extended family at work making the whimsical human figures that will ultimately bear her name.

At the same time, the figure of the *maestro artesano* (master artisan) looms large in Mexico, particularly in places like Oaxaca where handicraft production is an important economic activity. There is a historical reason for this. After the Mexican Revolution (1910–1920), crafts that at one time had been anonymously produced for local markets became the target of intensive state-led development, in the service of both nationalism and rural economic development aimed at stemming migration from the countryside (García Canclini 2010; López 2010; Novelo 1976). These interventions altered how folk arts were evaluated both within and outside of Mexico. The creation of government agencies such as the National Fund for the Development of Arts and Crafts (FON-

ART), fairs, and national contests promoting handicrafts all contributed to the personalization of talent, as individuals were designated as "masters" of various craft traditions. Beyond state institutions, the global art market—driven by collectors, museums, private foundations, and companies—has also favored specialization and individualization (Cant 2019). Indeed, one of the most publicized exhibits of Mexican folk art in recent decades was *Great Masters of Mexican Folk Art,* which toured the United States between 2001 and 2004 and was sponsored by the Mexican bank Banamex, as well as by Corona Extra, Mexico's National Council for Culture and Arts (CONACULTA), Tequila Herradura, and Aeroméxico (Coffey 2018). The traveling exhibition and its accompanying book (Fernández de Calderón and Sarmiento 2021) introduced audiences throughout North America to over one hundred men and women artisans considered exemplary of their craft. Today, individual authorship is considered intrinsic to high-end Mexican craft objects, while other labor along the production chain often goes unrecognized.

Mezcal-making in Oaxaca is increasingly organized and validated in ways similar to folk art as it enters the commercial market. And like wood carving or treadle-loom weaving, it is overwhelmingly associated with men. However, if one examines the complete process of mezcal-making, from an agave plant in the field to a bottle ready to be sold, more often than not it involves multiple people, including women. Nevertheless, mezcal-making retains a special category for the individual maker, the *maestro mezcalero,* who is considered the repository of the combined knowledge, technical skill, and palate that lends each finished mezcal its special character. This figure is akin to the chef in the culinary world. Women cook, but it is still overwhelmingly men who achieve chef status; and while there may be a whole cadre behind the scenes in the kitchen, the food's distinctiveness and artistry are ultimately the signature of the chef at the helm (Black 2021).

The tendency to attribute craft mezcal to a singular maker is reinforced through the connected mechanisms of marketing, tourism, and heritagization (Harvey 2008). For instance, it is common to include the *maestro mezcalero*'s name, and even signature, on bottle labels. Meanwhile, the mezcal tours that predominate are still mostly led by men and frame meeting the generally male maker as a highlight; tours are venues in which place, product, and maker align in such a way that consumers may easily identify the heritage-maker and the product—that is, the *maestro mezcalero* and his mezcal. These minor but illuminating details point to a value chain—the sequencing of value along a production chain—in which value inheres in authorship while other essential forms of labor are diminished. Women's contributions, unfortunately, do not always coincide with mezcal's public face. This holds true for women's work that is folded into their household duties, but also women's work that is performed as wage labor in *palenques*. Of course, not all women are rendered invisible within the value chain. In the next section I look at an opposing scenario: drawing attention to femaleness has become one of many value-adding strategies within the mezcal industry. How women actually fare in this context is another question altogether.

Gender as Value Adding

In 2015 I was doing fieldwork in Oaxaca when the story of an Indigenous, fourteen-year-old girl identified as Adela—no last name given—made local and national news for starting her own artisanal mezcal distillery in order to help out her economically struggling family (see, e.g., AIEDMX 2015; Rodriguez 2015). Nicknamed the "Niña Mezcalera" (Mezcal Girl) and touted by the media as the youngest-ever female producer, the girl turned out to be Adela Cruz Antonio from San Dionisio Ocotepec, a small Zapotec-speaking town about sixty-four kilometers from Oaxaca City. According to the report, she had launched her La Palenquerita (Little Distiller) brand as part of a school project, hoping that it could support her ailing father, who worked as a wage laborer in another distillery and had contemplated going to the United States to seek work. After winning first place in three regional competitions, the young *mezcalera* caught the attention of the state governor, who pledged 825,000 pesos (approximately US$52,000) in state funds to help commercialize her product. Meanwhile, the Oaxacan secretary of tourism and economic development made his own show of support by promising to include her in the National Mezcal Fair catalog, connect her with mezcal distributors, help her develop an export plan, and include her *palenque* on the state's planned mezcal route, then under development.

The feel-good nature of the story is undeniable; everyone that heard about the Niña Mezcalera marveled that a person so young could demonstrate such tenacity, and there were likely those who sought out her mezcal because of it. But while the producer's young age and desire to help her family were undoubtedly part of the appeal, these details do not fully explain why this story garnered such attention. After all, it is not uncommon to find boys this age working in *palenques*, out of familial obligation, financial necessity, or, more likely, a combination of the two. What makes the story noteworthy is that its young protagonist makes good mezcal *and* also happens to be a girl. The Oaxacan governor made a financial bet that if nothing else, his investment would yield a return in positive publicity for his contributions to both the industry and female empowerment.

How does gender become operationalized as part of craft mezcal's value proposition? Given that women's contributions tend to be overlooked or unacknowledged in the value chain, what are we to make of cases like La Palenquerita—where female labor and initiative are not only recognized but financially rewarded? La Palenquerita is certainly not the only brand to leverage gender to sell mezcal. Nevertheless, when brand identity is tied to gender, it often has more to do with the brand owners/marketers themselves than with the mezcal's production.

For instance, in the state of Guerrero, which neighbors Oaxaca, two female researchers turned entrepreneurs are marketing a line of artisanal mezcal under the name Las Mujeres del Mezcal y del Maguey de México (Women of Mezcal and Maguey of Mexico). Everything about their product—its name, narrative, and imagery—is explicitly woman centered, even though some of their mezcal is produced by husband-and-wife teams and some credited to a single *maestro mezcalero* (Flash 2021). Likewise, Mexico City native Cecilia Rios Murrieta founded her La Niña del Mezcal (Mezcal Girl) brand in 2011, after discovering mezcal on a trip to Oaxaca several years prior.[3] La Niña del Mezcal references the nickname bestowed on Rios Murrieta by others in the industry, ostensibly because she stood out among her mostly male peers. Its bottle is distinguished by its label, which has an all-black silhouette of a young woman with a contrasting, colored bow around her neck, an image reminiscent of a Victorian cameo (see La Niña del Mezcal, n.d.).

Not to be left out, the world of high fashion has continued its descent on Oaxaca, with *Vogue* jumping on the mezcal bandwagon by publishing numerous stories about the spirit. Several recent articles have featured artful shots of mezcal bottles, cocktails, and impeccably coiffed people in colorful yet tastefully minimal Oaxacan settings (see, e.g., Martineau 2015b; Schechter 2021). In addition to contributing to Oaxaca's ongoing folkloric gentrification, *Vogue*'s mezcal coverage also skews toward women in the industry. This is perhaps not surprising, given the magazine's target audience of affluent, trend-setting women—a demographic primed to be the latest craft mezcal consumers. In particular, *Vogue* has lavished attention on the infinitely Instagrammable Yola Mezcal, a female-run business that espouses women's empowerment as its central tenet (see, e.g., Gimmel 2021; Hartman 2016; E. Taylor 2018). The *Vogue* coverage has caused other media outlets such as the *New York Times* and *Bon Appétit* to also take notice.

The face behind the name is Mexico City native Yola Jimenez, who, along with Swedish recording artist and model Lykke Li and American chef and stylist Gina Correll Aglietti, founded Yola Mezcal in 2015. The brand purportedly uses Jimenez's grandfather's recipe to distill mezcal at a family property she inherited in San Juan del Río, an Indigenous Oaxacan community renowned for its craft mezcal. While Yola Mezcal ultimately generated substantial buzz thanks to its high-society and celebrity connections, it did so under the veneer of women helping women. Look no further than its website landing page, which, as of September 2022, included the brief brand statement, "Founded and run by women, Yola Mezcal's all female hand-bottling facility offers direct pay, and we are proud to promote autonomy and economic independence for our partners in Oaxaca and across borders" (Yola Mezcal, n.d.). Yet despite this platitude, it is not evident how employing women in a bottling facility (as opposed to in other forms of wage work) equates to economic independence, or how this particular type of work differs from that at other distilleries that also utilize women for the same task.

Nevertheless, what these cases do demonstrate is how gender is self-consciously deployed as part of mezcal's value proposition. This phenomenon is obviously not unique to mezcal. Mezcal, like all processed foods, is a value-added product. My use of the term *processed* follows Rebecca Dare, Håkan Jönsson, and Hans Knutsson (2013): it indicates, simply, that a raw commodity (agave) is transformed into a processed product (mezcal) through the use of materials, labor, and technology, all of which add value. Yet the authors emphasize that especially in the realm of small-scale food production (including craft and artisanal food), "culture" is a critical but often overlooked aspect of value adding; culture ultimately imbues food products with the meanings and associations that create our desire to consume them. In particular, the marketing of heritage and artisanal foods relies on culturally mediated emotions that ascribe value by associating products with specific places, social groups, and histories. In doing so, these "practices differentiate and have been developed in counter to the dominant food system in order to create competitive advantage" (Dare, Jönsson, and Knutsson 2013, n.p.).

Accordingly, competitive advantage is constituted in relation to the societal attitudes and politics of the time. Qualities that once may have proved to be a liability for a product can transform into value-adding qualities over time. This is clearly illustrated by the current global demand for Native or Indigenous food products, such as quinoa (Seligmann 2022) or pinole (Littaye 2016), which in the not-so-distant past were overlooked or even stigmatized by non-Indigenous consumers. Today, so-called ancient or traditional foods are part of an emerging economy at the forefront of discussions of climate change, biodiversity, and food sovereignty. Mezcal checks many of the same boxes due to its association with rural Indigenous communities. Changing ideologies regarding gender and women's roles in society also affect the value we place on certain goods and services, and ethical consumerism is seen as a mechanism for correcting historical legacies of both racism and gender inequality.

It should also be noted that women-made products—not just products marketed to women (e.g., the aforementioned pink mezcal)—have gained in value as part of a global movement of female entrepreneurship. There is no denying that women's growing disposable income and visibility as a market segment are partially driving this change. But supporting female entrepreneurs has also become a viable form of economic diplomacy as well as a perceived social good. This is part of a larger project of women's empowerment in developing countries that is "referred to as 'smart economics' and is increasingly motivated by reasons of economic growth, rather than by women's rights or justice as ends in themselves" (Lauri and Bäckström 2019, 869). Writing about the role of women and girls in foreign policy, Gayle Tzemach Lemmon (2012) adds that not only does supporting female entrepreneurs spur economic growth, it is tantamount to achieving political stability, particularly in conflict-prone regions.

Yet market-driven approaches to gender equality and women's development are not without their problems. One concern is that feminist values have been transformed into "popular culture, marketing strategies, and commodities" under twenty-first-century capitalism (Lauri and Bäckström 2019). Feminist scholar Angela McRobbie (2009) asserts that the process by which the material struggles and gains of women in previous decades are reduced to digital images and sound bites contributes to no less than the "undoing of feminism" itself. From this perspective, contemporary discourses of women's empowerment, self-care, self-esteem, personal responsibility, and so forth serve as vehicles for accelerating capitalist consumption rather than addressing the underlying societal forces that produce gender inequality in the first place.

In an industry that has been scrutinized for its transparency, craft mezcal brands that have women's empowerment at the core of their value proposition raise serious questions. To begin with, how are different women's contributions to mezcal-making accounted for and compensated? Within this global sisterhood, glossed as "women in mezcal," there is little acknowledgment of the tremendous social and economic gap between the women who possess the resources to found or operate mezcal companies and the women whose labor enables production on the ground; these women's distinct positions within the nested racial and class hierarchies of Mexico and a Global North/South divide means that they do not all share the same possibilities for claiming space in an industry that is still male dominated. Cases like Yola Mezcal exemplify free-market or "hegemonic" feminism as described by Hester Eisenstein (2009). She argues that by equating wage work with women's liberation, a global elite benefits from the exploitation of women's labor. Furthermore, it is US working-class women and women of color as well as women in the Global South who constitute this labor force. Consider what Yola Mezcal's three high-profile founders stand to gain in both money and cultural capital in comparison to the female wage workers in their employ.

Women in Mezcal

Women have always participated in mezcal-making in some way or another, even if their work has largely gone unacknowledged (Pardo Nuñez and Ángeles Carreño 2021). This is part of a larger pattern of craft production in Oaxaca, and Mexico more generally, and in this way mezcal might be more akin to folk arts than to other local comestibles. Over time, one-of-a-kind ceramics, textiles, and wood carvings become associated with one gender or the other, or with named, individual makers, particularly as *artesanías* make their way into global and fine arts markets. Like so many other forms of work in rural Oaxaca, crafts—and craft mezcal—are often embedded in wider systems of household production that cannot be reduced to a single individual, male or female.

At the same time, there is a growing movement to bring more visibility to women in mezcal, particularly on the marketing side of the value chain. In Oaxaca these efforts have been spearheaded by Graciela Ángeles Carreño, Sandra Ortíz Brena, and Silvia Philion, three female entrepreneurs who have strategically used their positions as partners in successful mezcal bars and brands (Real Minero Mezcal, In Situ

Mezcalería, and Mezcaloteca, respectively) as a platform for advocacy. Uniting in 2022 as a collective under the name Mujer Agave, they have organized forums and conferences where women can share their stories and expertise. It is also thanks to them that the first, and so far only, book to take a gender perspective on mezcal, *Miradas femeninas desde el mezcal,* was published in 2021, notably well over a decade after the boom began. This prompts the question of why it took so long to see coverage of women in the field. They and other women have also been outspoken on some of the industry's more contentious issues, from environmental degradation to mezcal categories defined through the mezcal certification process (Nabhan and Suro Piñera 2023).

Nevertheless, despite such advocacy efforts, disentangling a feminist politics from market-driven production has proven difficult. In a seeming contradiction, women are still largely invisible in mezcal, even as "woman owned" and "woman produced" are among the qualities that add value to the product. Rather than mutually exclusive phenomena, they are, in fact, two sides of the same gender-inequity coin. Gender exceptionalism—by which I mean the tendency to view women working in mezcal as situationally rare or unique—demands invisibility in order to generate value in the contemporary marketplace. Craft mezcal in the modern era is also about hierarchies of value. Masculinity is overdetermined in its market, while women are oversold in its marketing. Both of these translate into value propositions.

It is easy to spot and call out the bro culture that pervades the mezcal world, where there is no shortage of "wealthy, white, straight men" buying, branding, touring, tasting, and publicly opining on mezcal. Declaring a mezcal "balls to the wall" and suitable for a fine cigar in the company of "your lady friend" parallels performances of masculinity that center on the consumption of other alcoholic drinks such as whiskey (but not white wine!). In fact, one US company proudly rebukes critiques of whiskey culture's "toxic masculinity" by adopting the phrase as its own company name: Toxic Masculinity Whiskey. Such self-conscious branding is rooted in what is conventionally regarded as sexist behavior and attitudes toward women. It points to a marketing paradigm in which a "take it for yourself" attitude is the expression of the adventurous and sometimes aggressive position that bro culture exemplifies. Nevertheless, this chapter has shown that there are other, perhaps less noticeable, ways in which the mezcal market disadvantages women, even in its apparent celebration of them.

Notably, the global craft market now puts particular value on women's work that is tied to ethics of equality and social justice. Thus, we see a proliferation of mezcal projects and products promoting female labor as an unequivocal force for social and economic betterment—something we should all feel good about. The question we must always ask is: who benefits within this value proposition, and how? This requires thinking about women in mezcal not as a monolithic category but instead through an intersectional lens, considering how women are differently situated within the industry along racial/ethnic and class lines. It is to understand the position of women like Reyna Sánchez and the Niña Mezcalera in the mezcal market as distinct from that of women with greater access to forms of economic and social capital.

Too often, the inclusion of women requires that their circumstances be extraordinary; otherwise, they simply go unrecognized. This corresponds to the logic of what Gilles Deleuze and Félix Guattari (2009) termed "latent capitalism," where in order to become competitive in the marketplace, people must consistently differentiate themselves in that market. In the case of Reyna Sánchez, her uniqueness makes her a marketable resource but also drives her social exclusion. This is why gender exceptionalism adds value in the male-dominated world of mezcal. It creates the idea of scarcity, which itself becomes the basis of a demand. But we should not conflate creating value with valuing women; that is another project, one that requires the systematic rethinking of how we view and count women's labor not only in the making of mezcal, but in all other forms of production.

6 | Can Mezcal Save a Village?

In 2014, US National Public Radio (NPR) aired a segment on its *Planet Money* series provocatively titled "Can Mezcal Save a Village?" The story was a follow-up to a broadcast from ten years earlier, 2004, that had speculated as to whether Oaxaca's then-incipient mezcal industry represented a viable alternative to emigration from the region's many impoverished rural communities (NPR 2004, 2014). The 2014 story focused on two cousins from San Cristóbal Lachirioag, a Zapotec-speaking community of a little over one thousand residents in the mountains of Oaxaca's Sierra Norte. In 1999, Edgar González Ramírez and Elisandro González Molina both migrated to California's Silicon Valley, with the dream of saving enough money to someday return to their village to start a mezcal business, creating local jobs in the process. Throughout the segment, the radio journalist cautiously yet optimistically portrays the cousins' quest to develop their mezcal brand, Tosba, as illustrative of mezcal's potential to revitalize stagnant rural communities and stem out-migration.

The folks at NPR were not the only ones to speculate about the socioeconomic impact of mezcal on Oaxaca's rural sector. The state of Oaxaca began to prioritize the development of the mezcal industry during the tenure of Governor Gabino Cué Monteagudo (2010–2016), who spearheaded a new, if controversial, state-sponsored tourist route focused on mezcal, in addition to providing financial packages and certification training for small producers to help them upgrade their *palenques* (mezcal distilleries) and, ideally, prepare them to enter the commercial market. Today, international and Mexican entrepreneurs alike flock to Oaxaca with dreams of starting their own mezcal companies, and new brands and mezcal-related businesses seem to appear—some only to disappear—overnight. But has the mezcal boom lived up to the promise of alleviating rural precarity in what remains one of the poorest and most Indigenous states in the country?

"Mezcal still felt brand new in 2009," observed food and beverage writer Chantal Martineau (2015a, 170) a few years into the boom. She was evidently referring to its newness as a consumer good, but I interpret this sense of newness to also include the world of possibilities mezcal represented. At the outset of my research, in 2011, one of mezcal's most-anticipated success stories was the creation of economic opportunities in the rural sector, which would allow people to remain in or return to their hometowns. A hopeful narrative that things *must* be improving for families involved in agave farming and mezcal production was voiced by many, from visiting NPR journalists to brand owners themselves. Indicators of capital flow into communities—shiny new trucks and home improvements of various sorts—were held up as proof that people were prospering and staying put, choosing rural life over a migrant existence in other parts of Mexico or farther away in the United States. And it was not only Oaxaca. That same year, the *New York Times* ran a story that challenged the idea that earning a living in rural Mexico was no longer viable; it described how a growing market for Mexican distilled spirits was prompting people to stay in their home communities in the Jalisco Highlands to farm agave and make tequila (Cave 2011).

Amid an interview in 2015, Hipócrates Nolasco Cancino, then president of the Mexican Regulatory Council for Mezcal Quality (COMERCAM), asked me whether I had any data that would support claims of rural economic growth and declining out-migration rates (I did not).[1] He, like other influential people I had met in the mezcal world, believed in the power of market growth to ameliorate impoverished rural conditions. This belief reflected a trend by large and small companies alike to revisit craft work as a sustainable, economically viable form of production for rural stakeholders, including artisans themselves, who have stood to gain the least historically within the product value chain (Klamer 1996). Similar hopes had been pinned to the development of rural craft industries at earlier points in Mexico's history, without such desired effects transpiring (Novelo 1976). But many within the mezcal industry clung to a newer ethos of social entrepreneurship, in which "compassionate capitalism" is a means to foment social justice and well-being through economic activity (Rajak 2011). From this perspective, market-driven development projects may be a force for good if properly implemented. The COMERCAM president sought proof that mezcal was one such vehicle.

Can mezcal, in fact, "save a village" by reversing the long history of economic marginalization and out-migration in Oaxacan communities? This chapter seeks to reframe rather than answer this question, which simply assumes that rural regions are in decline while positing the growth of the mezcal industry as a way to alter this trajectory. The cases presented below, in fact, suggest otherwise. Importantly, these arrangements neither preclude migration nor pose the rural sector as a self-contained developmental problem that is constituted outside of regional, national, and international flows of capital and labor. In fact, the success of mezcal producers depends heavily on the social and capital networks fostered through migration and other forms of circulation between localities that are rural, urban, and everything in between. These examples are by no means exhaustive of the range of individual and community experiences. However, they illustrate a deeply intertwined relationship between the rural and the urban, one that the mezcal market depends on and that is overlooked when we create such superficial, circumscribed boundaries.

A Walk in the Clouds

The NPR stories and other media coverage of Tosba turned Edgar González into somewhat of a celebrity in the mezcal world. But the headlines that make for compelling journalism do not always convey the complexity of the situations described. In González's case, mezcal was what brought him back to his home village of San Cristóbal Lachirioag—but it was also the reason he left for the United States in the first place. Craftwork has been a strategy for economically developing the Mexican countryside since the 1910 Revolution (see Novelo 1976). But rather than demonstrating how craft mezcal can "save a village," we might better interpret González's path to mezcal producer as indicative of a new rurality, one that is more invested in global interconnectedness than ever before.

I initially learned of the two NPR segments not while listening to the radio but while visiting the Tosba *palenque* in San Cristóbal Lachirioag. Elisandro González, the cousin also featured in the 2014 story, mentioned it in passing as we took a lunch break after a morning of learning about and preparing the ingredients used to make the brand's *mezcal de pechuga* (mezcal distilled with a chicken or turkey breast). I was there with a small group of US mezcal aficionados to participate in a mezcal "boot camp" through Experience Agave, a company that offered mezcal/tequila educational tours in Oaxaca and elsewhere (Experience Agave, n.d.). During our intensive two-day visit, we learned about the entire production process as well as the local community and ecosystem (see figure 6.1). We also heard how Tosba came into existence.

I never would have made a connection between Keanu Reeves and artisanal mezcal, even though celebrity branding is becoming commonplace (Hello, George Clooney!). But when I finally met up with Edgar González a few weeks later in a café in Oaxaca City to fill in more of the details, the first thing he asked me was whether I had ever seen *A Walk in the Clouds*, a 1995 film starring the Hollywood actor. It was a fictional story about a soldier (played by Reeves) returning home to California from World War II. In search of work on his way to Sacramento, he meets a woman who is heading home from college to help with the grape harvest at her family's vineyard. Shot on location in California's Napa and Sonoma wine country, the movie highlights the region's natural beauty and viticulture. Edgar saw the movie in 2002 during his last year of university study in Oaxaca City, where he was finishing a degree in information systems. While the film focuses on a romance between its main characters, it was the romance of the landscape and winemaking tradition that really captivated him. "I just really liked the way that the people lived, surrounded by the vineyards, making wine," he said. The image of joyful villagers coming together to stomp grapes in giant vats became stuck in his head, and he wondered how such a scene of communitas might be replicated in Lachirioag.

Grapes were not climatically suited to Oaxaca's Sierra Norte, but there were wild agaves on his family's lands. He knew that historically mezcal had been made in the region, although no one in Lachirioag was currently doing so. He looked into what it would take to start farming agaves and acquire the necessary equipment to make mezcal. Even though he had a university degree (the only one among his five siblings), the job offers he had received in Oaxaca City generally paid just over US$400 per month. Edgar thought back to 1997, when he had temporarily migrated to the United States and worked in an Italian restaurant in Silicon Valley, putting in twelve-hour days at US$9.75 per hour. The calculation was not difficult. The only way to save up the money needed to finance his project was to return to the Unites States.

Back in Silicon Valley, he found work as a dishwasher in another Italian restaurant and moved in with his cousin Elisandro, who had left for the United States right after high school. The San Jose business employed a number of Oaxacan migrants, including four others from the cousins' village. Edgar worked his way up through the ranks at the restau-

Figure 6.1 Edgar González explains his distillation process at his *palenque* in San Cristóbal Lachirioag, Oaxaca. Photo by author.

rant, making salads and pizzas, and eventually graduating to cooking, all the while attending English-language classes in his off-hours. Each year he sent home a part of his earnings to buy equipment as well as agave, putting in several thousand plants annually, until he and Elisandro, with whom he had now joined forces, decided to return to Mexico in 2007 to move their business plan forward.

The cousins temporarily parted ways. Elisandro headed off to Guadalajara to study international business, while Edgar grappled with the fact that despite now having raw materials and equipment, he still did not know how to actually make mezcal. He went to the village of Santo Domingo Albarradas, which was becoming known for its artisanal mezcal, including one produced for Del Maguey. He asked around and eventually found a man who made mezcal locally and was willing to come to Lachirioag to help Edgar set up his still and train him to use it properly.

Mastering the technical elements of distillation and learning how to taste and experience mezcal as his target consumers might turned out to have a steep learning curve. After about a month of working with the acquaintance from Santo Domingo Albarradas, Edgar felt confident enough to produce mezcal on his own. He took a sample from an early batch with him when he went to the Mexican Regulatory Council for Mezcal Quality (COMERCAM) office in Oaxaca City to initiate the certification process. There he was told that he first needed to have a chemical analysis done to ensure that the mezcal complied with safety and denomination of origin (DO) guidelines. The chemist at the lab who performed the analysis serendipitously had worked with the distillery in Santiago Matatlán that produced Los Danzantes mezcal, a successful artisanal brand started in 1996 by twins Gustavo and Jaime Muñoz and served in their destination eatery of the same name in Oaxaca City. So Edgar tried to take it as a learning moment when she told him that his mezcal tasted, in his retelling, "bad, truly bad. Horrible, actually." She spent two hours explaining what he had done wrong, not the least of which included overfermenting his agave mash. He returned to his *palenque* more determined than even to perfect his product, and by 2011 he had fully certified mezcal ready to sell. He recalled that as the mezcal rush began, outsiders approached him about making mezcal for them to resell under their own brands. But the price of thirty pesos per liter they were offering convinced him that he could do better by selling under his own brand, which he had named Tosba.

In the meantime, Elisandro took advantage of a short stint in Guadalajara to learn as much as he could from the tequila industry, meeting with representatives from the Tequila Regulatory Council (CRT) and enrolling in trainings and workshops. He and Edgar had already agreed that their primary market would be US consumers, starting with restaurants and businesses in and around San Jose. He found cork and bottle suppliers, and a French friend living in Mexico put him in touch with an industrial designer back in France who agreed to design Tosba's label—minimalist and gender neutral, with subdued colors and silver font, so as to appeal widely to an international professional class. Armed with a product design and business plan, he returned to San Jose, eventually finding work in an upscale Mexican bistro. Proximity to multiple city bars and restaurants allowed Elisandro to move into his newest role as a mezcal brand ambassador, and he set to work shopping Tosba around to get it on area drink menus.

The cousins' industriousness and division of labor paid off. By the time I met them in 2015, Tosba was one of the artisanal brands I frequently heard referenced by others in the mezcal industry—not only for its excellent product but also for its unique story and the genuine amicability of its founders. Edgar was self-supporting from mezcal sales and contemplating branching out into coffee growing.[2] He now had five employees working with him at the *palenque,* some from a different Indigenous village and language community, earning 150 pesos (around US$9.50) per day, plus meals. Tosba was still growing, but, like the NPR journalists who had interviewed the cousins in prior years, Edgar remained cautiously optimistic about mezcal's ability to provide a livelihood for him and his family.

From *Paquetería* to Mezcal Brand

I met Armando Isidro Aquino at a mezcal tasting course hosted by the Technological University of the Central Valley of Oaxaca in Zimatlán, about twenty-five kilometers to the south of Oaxaca City. The two-day class brought together people from throughout the industry—local brand and business owners, chefs, and other hospitality workers—with the objective of teaching participants how to "appreciate and effectively communicate mezcal's technical and sensorial properties." The class was led by a *maestro catador* (master taster) from Guadalajara, Juan Bernardo Torres, a member of the Mexican Academy of Tequila, Wine, and Mezcal Tasters. The lectures, demonstrations, and tastings featured a handful of local mezcals, including A Medios Chiles (At Half Chiles), a brand founded by Aquino. Apart from its witty name, a Mexican colloquialism that refers to the state of being buzzed but not entirely drunk, the mezcal brand caught my attention because of its origins. During the class's opening remarks, Aquino told the audience that A Medios Chiles was a "migration story," one that unfolded in an interview a few weeks later.

The fifty-three-year-old Aquino grew up in San Pablo Huixtepec, a town not too far from the town of Zimatlán, in the district of the same name. Much of the community still farmed during his childhood, and he and his nine siblings helped his parents and grandparents cultivate traditional subsistence crops as well as tomatoes destined for local markets; other neighbors produced mezcal, which he recalled being consumed by people during their brief breaks while working in the fields. Like many Mexicans of his generation affected by the 1980s economic crisis, Aquino left to find work in the United States, eventually landing in the Northern California town of Seaside, not far from Monterey. There he joined a growing population of Oaxacans from his hometown of Huixtepec and elsewhere, most of whom worked in agriculture, construction, or service industries.

Aquino saw a demand and business opportunity in the Oaxacan migrant community, where people longed for foods and other products not easily obtained in the United States. In 1990, he and another brother also in California started up a *paquetería,* a courier service catering to Mexican transnational communities (see Gálvez 2021). They mostly transported familiar Oaxacan foods such as dried chiles, cheese, dried meats, *tlayudas* (large, semitoasted tortillas), mole, chocolate, and mezcal, but also documents, money, photos, clothing, and other household goods. Aquino described their cargo as *productos de nostalgia,* products that were tied to migrants' memories of their home communities. At the time, many of these things would have been impossible or prohibitively expensive to ship via the post office or commercial delivery services—not to mention that *paqueterías* were a means of cultural and geographic connection, as anthropologist Alyshia Gálvez (2021) observes, a way of "humanizing a dehumanized food system."

Business was brisk, and Aquino's brother found himself flying back and forth to Oaxaca twice a week to fill requests. In the meantime, Aquino returned to Mexico, where he studied agricultural engineering at the Chapingo Autonomous University, a well-regarded agricultural university in the state of Mexico, and went on to work in the coffee and later heirloom maize industry. His brother stayed in Seaside to manage the US side of the business, while Aquino and other family members managed things on the Oaxaca side.

By the late 1990s, border controls had become stricter, even as NAFTA proponents maintained that the agreement would stimulate free trade between the United States, Mexico, and Canada. Aquino noted that the goods that *paqueteros* commonly passed across the border were being more frequently detained or confiscated. The brothers decided that it was time to formalize their business and set up a limited liability company (LLC), Aromas y Sabores de Mi Tierra (Aromas and Flavors of My Homeland), in California, while also creating a partner export company in Mexico. One challenge with becoming a registered business was that they could no longer import food and mezcal that did not meet US federal regulations. In the past they had purchased mezcal in Huixtepec and elsewhere, but often these mezcals were not certified for sale or export. They reasoned that it would be easier to become a California distributor for a mezcal that was already commercially available.

They approached Pedro Mateo López, founder of Benevá, one of a handful of Oaxaca's early commercial brands, who agreed to the arrangement.

In the meantime, Aquino had been working on an idea for a mezcal brand of his own. During his time in Seaside, he had seen that there was a market for mezcal not only among his Mexican compatriots but also within Monterey County's wealthy enclaves. Having worked with specialty coffee and heirloom maize varieties, Aquino also saw that the market was trending in favor of local, nonindustrial food and drink. He began the process of registering his brand name with the Mexican Institute of Industrial Property (IMPI). Experience from his days as a *paquetero* came in handy in identifying several small producers in the districts of Zimatlán and Sola de Vega, including in Huixtepec, who agreed to produce mezcal under his new label. When the owner of Benevá met an untimely death in 2011, shot and killed by a cousin over a property dispute, Aquino was already well underway with his own mezcal venture, having launched A Medios Chiles in 2009, at the outset of the "mezcal rush" (Greene 2017). By the time I met him in 2015 at the mezcal tasting course, he had begun dedicating himself full time to building the brand under his Oaxaca-based company Casa Ancestral, whose products were now in both national and international markets.

Stories Untold

Tosba and A Medios Chiles are mezcal brands that have managed to establish themselves in a competitive marketplace. But more than that, they represent self-narratives of success that become more powerful with each retelling, shaping our understanding and expectations of mezcal's potential to create economic opportunity across the spectrum. They are undeniably great stories, and the ones everyone likes to hear. Nevertheless, we should remind ourselves why they resonate so strongly. One reason is that they lend credence to the belief that the global demand for mezcal may ultimately generate sustainable livelihoods, especially in rural areas. But as Raymond Williams (1975) theorized, a pastoral existence tends to take on an idyllic tint when viewed from the city. For every story of the migrant able to go back to or stay in their hometown thanks to mezcal, there are countless more in which mezcal does not materialize as an economic salve.

One frequently overlooked or understudied aspect of the Oaxacan mezcal industry is the variety of work involved, which includes but is

Figure 6.2 A laborer cleans leftover agave fibers from a grinding stone. Photo by author.

not limited to women's unpaid labor. While the popular idea of a *maestro mezcalero* (master mezcal maker) working in a small family distillery making craft mezcal is a big part of the drink's appeal, it does not fully account for those who make up the labor chain. Predictably, as the production scale increases, so too does the reliance on wage labor. As others have noted, the tequila industry has long depended on agricultural laborers for the arduous work of harvesting agave plants (Bowen 2015; Martineau 2015a), jobs that are not particularly well remunerated. In the case of mezcal, even small family-run distilleries often depend on *chalanes* (helpers or assistants in manual labor) from harvesting to bottling and everything in between; both Tosba and A Medios Chiles relied on teams of paid workers to produce their mezcal, with the latter brand supplied by multiple *palenques* (see figure 6.2). And here is the crux of the matter: if not everyone can own and run their own successful mezcal businesses (spoiler: most cannot), then are the jobs and the related infrastructure they create lucrative enough to keep people from leaving and seeking work elsewhere?

My time doing participant observation in a small artisanal distillery in Tlacolula in 2013 suggests that there is not a simple answer to this question. Granted, with a population of over 16,500 people, Tlacolula is hardly a village. However, it serves as a major commercial hub for some of the biggest mezcal-producing communities in the district of the same name, and in that sense it is deeply tied to rural economies in its orbit. The distillery produced mezcal for five different brands, two belonging to the *palenque* owner himself, and all of which were certified for commercial sale, including in US and European markets. The owner's family was well established in the local mezcal industry and relatively well-off, and he himself had an engineering background. Because he lived in Oaxaca City and was frequently away, the palenque's day-to-day operation fell to a core group of five male employees, each of whom I got to know to varying degrees.

There was Tomás, who was my age and from Tlacolula.[3] He was the one the owner most trusted to make sure that everything that needed to get done was done, whether that was cutting agaves in the field, cleaning fermentation vats, or prepping the stills. His stocky, sturdy frame belied his soft-spoken nature and sensitive personality. Unlike most men his age, he did not have a wife or children. He explained to me as we cleaned out fermentation vats one day that he had lost his fiancée to a sudden cardiac arrest; he was still heartbroken, his eyes tearing up anytime he brought her up, which was often. There was Celestino, a gregarious, older man whom I placed in his early to midsixties. He had worked a variety of manual labor jobs throughout his life and struggled with drinking, a problem that was exacerbated by work in an alcohol distillery and that ultimately led to his dismissal before I got to know him well. Nacho, in his midforties, was arguably the brawn of the operation. Most days he could be found splitting giant agave hearts with an axe, loading and unloading the in-ground oven where they were roasted, or running behind the horse that pulled the giant stone wheel used to crush them. He had a fondness for muscle shirts and wore his long hair in a braid, covered with a wide bandanna; people frequently remarked that he resembled rock musician Carlos Santana, a point of pride for him. He also spoke flawless English, having previously spent over twenty years living in the United States, before a DWI arrest resulted in him being deported back to Mexico. He planned to stay at the distillery only as long as it took to save up money for a return trip north, where he had a friend waiting for him in Arizona.

The other two employees were brothers from San Lucas Camotlán, an Indigenous village of about 2,500 people in the Sierra Mixe region. They were among five of thirteen siblings currently residing outside of their home community, where their monolingual Mixe-speaking parents still farmed coffee. The older brother, Germán, thirty-three, had arrived first in Tlacolula, with dreams of starting a *tortillería* (tortilla manufacturer). In the meantime, he had landed a job in the distillery, where his brother Eliseo later joined him. Both were reserved and kept to themselves at work, so it took me by surprise when Eliseo asked, some months after we first met, whether I would be his *madrina* (godmother) for high school graduation.[4] Had he not asked, I would never have thought he was a high school student, due to his highly mature demeanor.

I found out that Eliseo had left San Lucas Camotlán when he was seventeen years old; he was now twenty and set to graduate. One motivation for coming to Tlacolula, in addition to finding work, was to complete high school. He initially worked as a masonry assistant, earning 500 pesos (US$40) per week, before joining the distillery crew where his brother was employed a few months later. The arrangement suited him well. The owner let him work half days so that he could attend classes, and his pay increased to 800 pesos ($65 US) per week. During his first year on the job, the owner took note of his unusual skill for numbers and attention to detail, shifting his duties away from more physical tasks to maintaining the distillation logs, testing sugar and alcohol levels, and overseeing orders and shipping. These tasks would ideally have been assigned to Tomás, who was older and more experienced, but Eliseo was the only one who knew how to use the business's computer, a skill he had recently learned in his classes.

Once he graduated, Eliseo transitioned to full time, and his weekly pay doubled to 1,600 pesos (US$130). By 2015, his pay had risen to 2,000 pesos (US$163) and he had earned the title of general manager. He told me that the going pay rate for a worker, not the owner, in a Tlacolula *tortillería* was roughly 1,200 pesos (US$98) weekly, while agricultural labor paid in the neighborhood of 250–350 pesos (US$20–28) per day. Though the *palenque* owner's somewhat volatile temperament put him (and everyone else, from what I observed) on edge, the work was steady, and the pay, by Oaxaca standards, was not bad, allowing him to cover his living expenses (e.g., food and rent), albeit expenses he would not have incurred living back in the village with his parents.[5]

But Eliseo viewed his job in the mezcal *palenque* as merely a means to an end, confiding in me his desire to get a college degree, perhaps in architecture or engineering. He enjoyed drawing cars, planes, and machinery, and had even designed an original prototype for a machine that would automatically put wax seals on mezcal bottles. The last time

I saw him, at the end of 2015, Eliseo, by then twenty-two, talked about buying land in Tlacolula so that one day he could build a home and perhaps farm the land or build a small business. Neither he nor his brother Germán envisioned a future in which they returned to farming in San Lucas Camotlán.

Eliseo and I remained in contact after I returned to the United States. But shortly after, I received a message from him indicating that he, too, had left Oaxaca. He was now 2,600 kilometers from home, living in Caborca, a midsize city in the northern state of Sonora. Caborca was a hub for industrial agriculture, and he was working in the fields, picking asparagus that would make its way to supermarkets across the United States. When I asked him why he had left the *palenque,* he said that the wages were higher in Sonora, even though the work and living conditions were admittedly difficult. Some months later, he contacted me again, this time from near the Tijuana–San Diego border, where he was hoping to cross. He still dreamed of college, he said, but it would have to wait until he could save money. Mezcal was part of his past, not his future, he concluded.

A New Rurality

The image of Mexico as a country of campesinos lingers in the popular imagination on both sides of the US-Mexico border, and for good reason. For much of its history, Mexico was a predominantly rural nation where livelihoods derived overwhelmingly from agriculture and associated petty craft industries, alongside resource extraction (primarily mining) in some regions. This began to change, however, during the mid-nineteenth and early twentieth centuries, as Mexico sought to modernize alongside other nations in the western hemisphere. During the dictatorial regime of President Porfirio Díaz, between 1876 and 1911, Mexico aggressively courted foreign investment and undertook a host of projects aimed at enlarging its industrial output and infrastructure. In the north, the mining sector and railroad system boomed, while new agribusiness technology and investment made farming more productive and efficient in the central and southern regions; at the same time, the creation of a modern banking system facilitated industrial activity, particularly investment by American companies (Hart 2006).

Modern Mexico's economic development benefited some but left many more behind. In the countryside, the ongoing consolidation of land in the hands of the elite fueled resentment among the rural poor, who became an even more readily disposable labor force. There is not space here to enumerate the many events and issues leading up to the 1910 Revolution. But agrarian reform was a key factor in the twentieth century's first major political and cultural revolution, enshrined in the figure of revolutionary leader Emiliano Zapata. The postrevolutionary powers that emerged from the conflict and that would ultimately coalesce into the Institutional Revolutionary Party (PRI)—the political party that would rule Mexico for the next seventy-two years—espoused an ideology of agrarian development, built on the demand for land redistribution.

Nevertheless, throughout the twentieth century Mexico experienced massive economic and demographic changes that did not promote the betterment, or even maintenance, of its rural sector, setting in motion a pattern of temporary and permanent rural out-migration. Even during its period of unprecedented economic growth between 1940 and 1970, the so-called Mexican Miracle, the Mexican state was unable to effectively invest in rural communities enough to counterbalance the prospect of higher wages in urban areas within Mexico and in the United States. Relative political stability and the implementation of import substitution industrialization after World War II created the conditions for rapid urbanization, population and per capita income growth, and general improvements in health and education (Alba and Potter 1986). Unfortunately, these outcomes were not experienced equally across Mexico, and regions like Oaxaca that were already on the geographic and economic periphery saw little by way of such post–World War II gains (Murphy and Stepick 1991).

In subsequent decades, Mexico's participation in NAFTA liberalized trade with the United States and Canada, flooding the country with cheap agricultural imports. One consequence of this was that peasant farmers—who had once been a symbol of agrarian reform during the first half of the twentieth century—found themselves playing a much-diminished role as contributors to the national food supply. Government efforts to offset the negative effects of NAFTA on agriculture—like the 1994 farm subsidy program PROCAMPO—ultimately benefited well-off farmers rather than economically struggling campesinos (Winters and Davis 2009). Well into the twenty-first century, scholars noted the link between neoliberal economic reforms and the abandonment of traditional farming by campesinos. For example, geographer Nathalie Gravel (2007, 77) observed that "in the new Mexican rural economy, unfavorable market conditions for agricultural products and the lack of support to small-scale productive activities act as incentives to cease operations and leave for the city, or even the U.S." States with the highest rates of out-migration—like Zacatecas, in central Mexico—came to symbolize a rural exodus, characterized by villages "mainly inhabited by the elderly, lined with empty houses that have been improved by remittances, and paved with roads that facilitate the holiday returns of families from the United States" (Bada and Fox 2022, 29).

Empty villages and fallow cornfields may have characterized earlier discussions of neoliberalism and globalization. However, scholars today are instead focused on what has been termed Mexico's "new rurality," arguing that rural areas are not necessarily declining (shrinking or dying out) but rather are taking on new characteristics due to transformations to their social and economic structure (Bada and Fox 2022; Robson, Klooster, and Hernández-Díaz 2019). Xóchitl Bada and Jonathan Fox (2022, 31) describe new rurality as a condition in which "agricultural income and rurality are now *delinked* due to the hybrid nature of rural spaces that increasingly combine rural geographies amidst semi-urban arenas for income generation." They argue that residents today exhibit a greater diversity of income-generating strategies that are "more dependent on political competition, internal and international migration dynamics, violent displacement, and the power shift in local governance from agrarian to municipal authorities" (31). These shifts have been accompanied by changing patterns of female labor participation, a shrinking birth rate and smaller family size, and greater access to education among younger generations (Robson, Klooster, and Hernández-Díaz 2019). Key here is that rural communities are no longer wholly dependent on agricultural livelihoods, while at the same time the diversification of the rural sector has made it possible for more people to eschew out-migration in favor of local income opportunities. Thus, rural communities are not poised to disappear—but they are undergoing significant economic, social, and demographic transformations.

The contemporary craft mezcal industry must be considered part of this new rurality. Farming for subsistence and exchange in local markets is still important in rural Oaxaca, but it is increasingly complemented or supplanted by other forms of economic activity. And while mezcal production is undisputedly agriculturally adjacent—it relies on agave, after all—its reorientation to external markets at home and abroad imbues it with characteristics distinct from other "on-farm" activities, such as subsistence farming or livestock raising, typical of the region (Robson, Klooster, and Hernández-Díaz 2019). Moreover, it is reliant on wage labor, foreign direct investment, migration, and various inputs (capital, technology, logistics, and infrastructure) from state and municipal authorities; in some locations, mezcal production may even play a role in the "strategic coexistence" shared by agriculture and the illicit drug trade (Pansters 2018).[6] Furthermore, mezcal is heavily based on rural-urban interaction, without which there would be virtually no market at all.

And this brings us to another important consideration: much of the craft mezcal available in the commercial market (e.g., the brands we see in stores, restaurants, and bars) is not actually made in the rural hinterland we often imagine—a place that is distinct, and perhaps cut off, from the urban—although that is part of the fantasy fueling mezcal tourism. Rather, it is produced by small businesses with paid employees in places that are directly connected to semi-urban regional hubs. Santiago Matatlán, for example, is less than twenty minutes down the highway from Tlacolula. Even though it retains elements of rural life such as farming, its residents engage in a variety of economic activities that include mezcal-making and tourism, but also things having nothing to do with any of the above; younger residents in particular commute to jobs or school in Tlacolula, Mitla, and Oaxaca City, and are increasingly pursing college educations.

Having established mezcal within Oaxaca's new rurality, then, I return in the final section of this chapter to the individual stories presented above. Not only do they illustrate the challenges and opportunities posed by this evolving rural condition, but they may also help us get closer to answering the question of whether mezcal can indeed "save a village," or, better yet, cause us to reframe the question altogether.

Rethinking Mezcal Livelihoods

Current studies of rurality and Oaxacan migration owe much to anthropologist Michael Kearney (1995a), whose work discussed transnational Indigenous Mixtec communities that formed in California, or "Oaxacalifornia" as it is sometimes called, in the last decades of the twentieth century (see also Cohen 2004; Fox and Rivera-Salgado 2004; Stephen 2007). Kearney brought attention not only to the ethnic and racial diversity of Mexican migrants, but also to the enduring cultural and economic relationships that characterize such cross-border communities. His mandate to reconceptualize the "peasantry" signaled a pivoting away from thinking of rural Oaxaca as a self-contained economic and social sphere to understanding it as a place fully integrated into the global political economy (Kearney 1996). For Kearney, transnationalism—migration being one dimension—was central to the formation of new rural subjects.

Even though Kearney stopped short of delinking rural livelihoods from agricultural production, his emphasis on transnational processes is nevertheless critical to the topic of mezcal. For one, to view mezcal production as an activity contained in rural or semirural areas is a fallacy. We have seen how the current market for mezcal is externally directed, heavily cultivating consumers who are geographically distributed across national and international urban areas—whether in Mexico City or New York City—many of whom now travel to Oaxaca so that they can experience mezcal terroir in situ in the same way wine connoisseurs travel to vineyards all over the world (Picard 2018). But we might also consider how being or becoming a *mezcalero,* including attaining the requisite knowledge and skill related to the craft, is shaped through transnational migration itself. This is to say nothing of the financial capital that is accrued by individuals working abroad and channeled back to Oaxaca to fund mezcal-making enterprises.

In the cases of both Tosba and A Medios Chiles, migration to the United States is a central theme in their origin stories. Edgar González went to the United States with the explicit aim of becoming a *mezcalero,* a goal that he saw as unobtainable if he stayed in Oaxaca. Meanwhile, the idea for A Medios Chiles came about when Armando Aquino was running his *paquetería* business and saw a growing demand for mezcal not only among fellow Oaxacans but also among non-Mexicans in California. As important as their US earnings were to establishing businesses back in Oaxaca, so, too, was their exposure to what economist Pankaj Ghemawat (2007) identifies as the various cultural, administrative, geographic, and economic distances associated with doing business in a foreign market. These distances may include everything from complicated transportation networks to restrictive import/export regulations, complex tax structures, a political regime's lack of openness to foreign products, and insular cultural preferences. Critically, these distances imply that value is still heavily located in places outside of the actual production of mezcal, contributing to value-chain inequity. On the one hand, Tosba and A Medios Chiles brand owners' time working and living in California gave them insight into their market, precisely among the more affluent, urban consumers who have become key to mezcal's success. On the other hand, these experiences fostered an awareness that the distances involve significant inequity.

But these cases illustrate more than just the cultivation of a business acumen; they illustrate the role of migration in the formation of cosmopolitan subjectivities—ways of being at home in the world that are not tied to just one place. Geographer Michael Woods (2018, 165) notes that while cosmopolitanism was once typically attributed to "elite, transnationally mobile, relatively privileged social actors, whose life-spaces are anchored in global cities," scholars have broadened the term to include "individuals who are not part of a cultural or economic elite, but whose lives involve the everyday negotiation of cultural difference and transnational mobility." The Tosba cousins and Armando Aquino certainly exemplify the latter, which may be further distinguished as an "unintended and lived cosmopolitanism," epiphenomenal to the migration trajectory itself (Beck and Sznaider 2010). Functional ability in more than one language, an ease in interacting with people from different class, racial, and cultural backgrounds, an appreciation for a variety of food and drink beyond the familiar: these were all qualities they developed living outside of their communities of origin, qualities that we tend to associate with a well-traveled, educated global citizenry. To utilize the examples given here, it is the person in the village who is equally equipped to prepare a meal of Italian ravioli or *tejón* (coatimundi), or the one in the tasting class who knows how to pair glassware and food to best showcase mezcal's flavors and aromas. In other words, González and Aquino came to resemble their would-be clientele more than if they had never left Oaxaca in the first place. This allowed them to shape their brands and products accordingly.

These cases suggest that transnational migration can play a role in developing a competitive advantage or cosmopolitan outlook that leads to success in the mezcal industry back home. Nevertheless, we should ask whether these stories are the exception rather than the norm. For instance, after Aquino finished telling me how he started A Medios Chiles, I asked him whether he thought that the industry was going to attract other migrants back home to Oaxaca. "Here? No, I don't think so." He continued:

> Those examples that they give when they talk about mezcal, that people left, saved a bunch of money, and then returned to start a business, well that's maybe one out of a hundred. That's to say it's not most people's experience. But it's in the government's interest to say that. "Look at these entrepreneurs, they were poor, they didn't have anything, but they made a lot of money

> and they returned to start a business." The message serves them, mezcal is serving a higher purpose because it's keeping people from migrating . . . but believe me, even with the economic conditions being as they are in California, for many people it's still better there than being here [in Oaxaca].

He was clearly skeptical of political discourse that shifted the burden of development from the state to the individual, acknowledging that his own pathway to entrepreneurship was unique and unobtainable for most. His was a combination of luck and timing, but also the ability to accumulate capital from another business venture, his access to higher education, and his previous experience working in coffee, another agricultural commodity industry.

He also pointed out another important distinction, something he shared with Edgar González. Both owned their brands and had successfully certified their products for commercial sale. González owned Tosba and also made the mezcal sold under its label, while Aquino owned A Medios Chiles and contracted with local *palenques* to produce mezcal for his brand. In other words, neither was making mezcal to sell wholesale to another entity or individual that would, in turn, sell the product on the market and retain a large percentage of the profits. This raises the larger question of not just whether people in rural Oaxaca can sell mezcal, but also how much control they have over their product and its pricing within the market.

When we think of mezcal, we tend to think of an ideal scenario in which a small, rural producer is able to sell their mezcal for a fair price, either directly or indirectly (through a middleman), ensuring a secure living for their household. This romanticized vision does not capture what is truly occurring across the spectrum of production, which may range from a single campesino in a remote village to a college-educated engineer with a craft distillery in a semi-urban configuration like Tlacolula District. The rush on craft mezcal has witnessed outside buyers, with access to capital and other means, looking to buy mezcal at prices well below current market value. In fact, I encountered producers who were forced to sell their mezcal at a price that barely covered their costs. Others I met were initially so eager to ensure steady sales that they found themselves locked into multiyear contracts with individual brand owners or companies—the longest I recorded in my notes was thirteen years—which accounted for neither rising production costs nor mezcal's increased market value over the past decade.

Then there are those for whom mezcal work represents yet another form of rural wage labor, such as the workers from the Tlacolula distillery. Their salaries were higher than what they might have earned locally doing construction or agricultural labor, but not enough for them all to aspire to stay in them permanently; nor was there any pretension that someone would be able to break away and start their own mezcal business. Nacho was a prime example: he had no plans to stay in Mexico at all; the mezcal job was a necessary detour on his trip back north. Eliseo, too, despite having become incredibly knowledgeable about mezcal, to the point that on many days he appeared to be running the Tlacolula distillery single-handedly, ultimately decided that he would have a higher earning potential outside of Oaxaca as an agricultural laborer in northern Mexico and, later, in the United States.

Moreover, Eliseo's case represents another growing trend as it relates to mezcal and rural Oaxaca industries more generally, and that is internal migration within the state (Sandoval-Cervantes 2022). One thing that goes overlooked in describing Oaxaca as one of the poorest and most Indigenous regions of Mexico is that this status contains its own economic-ethnic hierarchy. This is to say that at the regional and municipal level, some places are better off economically than others, affecting both who migrates and to where (Alvarado Juárez 2008).

In some cases, these disparities map out along geographic territories that overlap with ethnolinguistic ones, as evidenced by the types of migrants who end up filling particular labor niches. A Zapotec colleague from Tlacolula pointed out to me one day as we strolled through its sprawling Sunday market that most of the young, male porters pushing through the narrow aisles with heavy loads were from the Sierra Mixe. They performed what was considered one of the most physically demanding yet lowest-paid jobs in the market. But as was the case for Eliseo, who was also Mixe, these jobs were economically preferable to what was available back home. One could speculate that the growth of mezcal production in select rural communities is creating another labor niche that, in turn, will stimulate internal migration. This is certainly possible as producers look for ways to both expand their operations and cut labor costs. Will the Mixe or other regions become a source of mezcal wage labor? Time will tell. But as I write this, rumors are circulating that the Zapotec-speaking village of San Juan del Río is building migrant housing to support the influx of workers staffing its numerous *palenques*, including one owned by the well-established brand Alipús.

I cite these details not because they are representative of all mezcal producers or producer communities. If anything, they suggest that the relationship between physical and economic mobility, rurality, and mezcal livelihoods is not reducible to a singular, linear trajectory. Likewise, we should put to rest the idea that decades of neoliberalism killed agriculture, simply gutting the rural sector in the process. Rather, we may observe a new rurality, where people continue to survive, and occasionally thrive, while undertaking a variety of activities that may be only tangentially related to agriculture, if they are related at all. Moreover, touting one industry as the solution for alleviating rural economic woes, with migration as a secondary effect, downplays the resiliency and creativity of rural Oaxacans exercising what Xóchitl Bada and Jonathan Fox (2022) describe as "the right to stay home" (see also Bacon 2013).

The reality that is mezcal, like most industries under late-stage capitalism, will create opportunities for some while exacerbating the social and economic challenges of others; as has been argued throughout this book, much depends on where one is positioned within the value chain. This conclusion is perhaps not surprising. But that has not dissuaded everyone from the popular media to government officials from engaging in the wishful thinking that somehow mezcal will be different. Rather than asking whether mezcal can save a village, we might instead examine its position within a new rural dynamic that still includes—indeed, may depend on—migration as part of its very success. And if there is truly a will to make mezcal a viable economic activity to significant numbers of rural Oaxacans, then we must first acknowledge that the interconnectedness of the global economic system does not neatly align with the complex realities of rural life. For even when the world is enamored with Oaxaca's products, there are chasms between production and consumption that involve more than just getting a product to a willing consumer.

CONCLUSION | Mezcal in a Twenty-First-Century Wonderland

> "No, I'll look first," she said, "and see whether it's marked 'poison' or not"; for she . . . had never forgotten that, if you drink much from a bottle marked "poison," it is almost certain to disagree with you, sooner or later.
>
> However, this bottle was not marked "poison," so Alice ventured to taste it, and finding it very nice (it had, in fact, a sort of mixed flavour of cherry-tart, custard, pine-apple, roast turkey, toffee, and hot buttered toast), she very soon finished it off.
>
> Lewis Carroll, *Alice's Adventures in Wonderland* (1865)

A mezcal enthusiast once explained his first encounter with the drink to me as "falling down the rabbit hole." His metaphor was drawn from Lewis Carroll's Victorian-era story about Alice, a young girl who is unwittingly transported to a surreal world that is as troubling as it is wonderful. It was the first but not last time I would hear someone narrate a mezcal experience this way, prompting me to revisit a story I had not thought about since childhood. I was surprised to discover how much Alice's adventures revolve around eating and drinking, revealing a penchant for consuming things that Carina Garland (2008) describes as Alice's "curious appetites."

But even more striking was the passage above, in which Alice is tempted by a bottle of some unknown substance, which may or may not be poisonous. In modern-day neoliberal market terms, we might say that the drink is subject to the "liability of foreignness." That is to say, it is a product that does not conform to what is easily sensed or known and therefore has costs associated with it (Eden and Miller 2004). If we extend this metaphor, mezcal, like the bottle in the story, had to overcome the liability of its foreignness, aided by its consumers' curious appetites. And those intrepid tasters willing to move beyond mezcal's past associations with poverty and Indigeneity, low quality, and other risks have been rewarded, like Alice, with something quite nice. It is remarkable how much Alice's description resembles the contemporary mezcal reviews referenced here—roast turkey, toffee, and hot buttered toast, indeed! Yet the bottle and its contents are not the only things that make up this wonderland. Magical elements such as a hookah-smoking caterpillar, mushrooms that can alter one's size, and playing cards with human heads and limbs equally contribute to Alice's sense of awe. The same may be said of Oaxaca, a place that has turned into something of a twenty-first-century wonderland, where curious travelers fall under the spell not only of its mezcal but also of its food, art, and culture. But as Carroll's young protagonist soon learned, the wondrous often generates its own frustrations and contradictions.

On a visit to Oaxaca City in March 2023, my first time there since before the 2020 global pandemic halted travel, I was shocked by how much the place had changed. The city buses and *colectivos* (communal taxis) that once barreled through the downtown area had been partially rerouted to peripheral streets, and there was talk of closing off a major downtown thoroughfare to create yet another pedestrian boulevard. Ostensibly this was a good thing; among the other Mexican and foreign tourists, I, for one, certainly relished the cleaner air and thinner traffic. But I was also aware that the city core was significantly cut off from public transportation. Unless they had cars (and good luck finding free parking), the service workers staffing the abundant hotels, coffee shops, restaurants, and boutiques would likely have a longer or more complicated commute. An apartment in a downtown complex that I rented for just under US$200 per month in 2015 was now going as a short-term rental for close to US$900, and the owner was now using the popular Airbnb online platform to connect with potential renters. To put this in perspective, as of April 2023, the Mexican government calculated the average monthly salary for the state of Oaxaca to be 3,490 pesos (approximately US$200) (Data México, n.d.).

The food scene, too, had radically changed. Some of the more popular restaurants now had wait lists and lines snaking down the sidewalk. One could assume that this was just a function of high tourist density in a circumscribed area of the downtown. However, Oaxaca City is also experiencing an influx of foreign expats and Mexicans from other areas of the country, notably Mexico City, who have relocated there permanently or semipermanently. Most seem content to be living their version of the good life, even as the city and some of the popular coastal towns become more crowded and expensive. One development in this trend is the presence of a younger demographic who have relocated to Oaxaca. They are there to pursue artistic dreams, work as digital nomads, and engage in other entrepreneurial activities. This led one elderly American woman I met on my last trip to complain, "Young people are ruining Oaxaca, I mean, they're making it totally unbearable!"

Their presence is felt not only in the central areas of the city but also in neighborhoods and satellite communities farther out. A Mexican friend who lived in a more working-class neighborhood on the city's south side recounted her frustration at recently trying to buy an empanada from a street vendor near her house. Arriving at the food stand, she noticed a "gringo" in line ahead of her who appeared to be not a tourist but a local, apparently living in the neighborhood. As she waited in line, her order of an *empanada de quesillo* on the tip of her tongue, the "gringo" bought the very last one. My friend reported walking home in defeat. A few days later, among Oaxaca City's endlessly colorful murals, I noticed some graffiti that read: "TURISTA GO HOME OAXACA ANTICAPITALISTA" (Go home tourist anticapitalist Oaxaca). The words stung as much as they resonated.

When I returned to Oaxaca in March 2024, the cracks in a system stressed by gentrification and climate change were more visible than ever. At least fifty forest fires had broken out in the state since the start of the year, and ongoing blazes had recently claimed the lives of five farmers from San Lucas Quiaviní who were trying to prevent the fire from reaching their village. Meanwhile, Oaxaca City was reaching a crisis point with regard to Mexico's water shortage; falling water tables and insufficient or failing wells meant that the city only had about one-fifth of its necessary water supply (Bruce 2024). City residents—some of whom reported going forty days or more without water in their homes—were increasingly outraged to find water being supplied to restaurants and hotels catering to tourists.

Oaxaca has historically been subject to waves of economic and cultural imperialism, from the Aztec who expanded their empire there in the mid-fifteenth century to the Spanish colonialists who succeeded them. But we should not forget that more recent influxes of artists, *jipis* (hippies), *chilangos* (colloquial for people from Mexico City), tourists, expats, and entrepreneurs of various stripes—the categories are not mutually exclusive—are also staking their own claims to the region's resources.

Meanwhile, Oaxacans are working to shape their economic destiny in a constantly shifting landscape in which they (like the mezcal they make) have been alternately disparaged and idealized. There is a cruel irony in watching something that was once stigmatized by the upper echelons of society later be popularized and monetized by some of the same people. Others have taken note. José Bolaños, a cartoonist for the local newspaper *El Imparcial de Oaxaca*, appended the following caption to his drawing in the October 6, 2015, issue of the paper:

> Antes si tomabas el MEZCAL, te tachaban de BORRACHO y pobre, pero ahora es "LA ULTIMA MODA" y todos son expertos en MEZCAL, y nos lo venden carísimo sólo porque son marcas de empresarios que ni siquiera son de Oaxaca.
>
> Before if you drank MEZCAL, they wrote you off as a poor DRUNK, but now it's the "LATEST FASHION" and they are all experts on MEZCAL, and they sell it at a high price only because they are brands by businesspeople who aren't even from Oaxaca. (my translation)

This is part of mezcal's history as highlighted in chapter 1. In the Spanish colonial system and its aftermath, non-European food and drink was considered low status, particularly beverages derived from agave; today, such comestibles are prized as authentic, prestige goods by a spectrum of consumers in and outside of Mexico. Hence, the story of mezcal is also the story of Oaxaca and Mexico, where we can see the same disparagements and celebrations extend into the global political economy: a bottle, a village, and a nation are all participating in conversation about their place in an increasingly connected world.

In the 1990s anthropologists became more attentive to the large-scale processes that are now collectively referred to as "globalization," and particularly to the culturally specific ways in which different groups mediated these processes (Appadurai 1996; García Canclini 1995; Kearney 1996). Part of the impetus for writing this book was that a product that I had only previously observed in a highly local context was suddenly popping up in unexpected places. Oaxacan mezcal was a textbook case of globalization, and serendipitously, I was able to witness the wholesale transformation of its status in real time. I also began to see mezcal as a proxy for the changes happening in Oaxaca, which I have watched become one of the most touted food and arts destinations in the world over the past thirty years. Importantly, these changes have not happened in a vacuum.

This book has shown how the popularity of mezcal and Oaxaca reflect wider twenty-first-century shifts in the global political economy. It is not just that all things, peoples, and places are subject to commodification. This may be true, but as Luc Boltanski and Arnaud Esquerre (2020) argue, the "enrichment economy" characterizing our current era imbues certain sectors—the arts, gastronomy, cultural heritage, tourism—with outsize value relative to others. And the value of these commodities, to a large degree, is located in their historical moorings. "Traditional" forms of production and the places where they persist are seen in a new, economically valuable light. The reemergence of the craft imaginary, the interdiscursive frameworks that translate expertise across artisanal and heritage products, and the development of gastronomic tourism discussed here are all indicators of the enrichment economy, with mezcal in Oaxaca now a central element in it. Mezcal's past, rooted in rural and Indigenous communities and nonmechanical production techniques, gave it a competitive advantage in the present market.

Still, we must contend with the fact that Oaxaca continues to lag behind much of the rest of Mexico in terms of most socioeconomic indicators. In this context the growth of a particular economic sector is notable. Mexico reported that the overall international sale of Oaxacan products in 2022 was up 24.7 percent from the previous year. The products bringing in the highest revenue were alcohol, presumably mezcal (US$86.7 million); followed by figs, pineapples, avocados, guava fruit and mangoes (US$40.9 million); and coffee (US$11.7 million) (Data México, n.d.). This indicates a heavy reliance on agricultural exports, which on the whole tend to command lower prices than manufactured goods. From a purely economic perspective, it hard to see the mezcal boom as anything other than a story of success. Add to this the continued growth of Oaxaca's tourism sector, which has defied the downward trend experienced in other Mexican states. A 2019 unsigned article in the *Economist* labeled Oaxaca as "pobre, pero sexy" (poor, but sexy) and asked, "Can Tourism Boost One of Mexico's Poorest States?" It went on to describe Oaxaca as "a bright exception," with the "number of foreigners flying into the capital, a colonial gem also called Oaxaca, soar[ing] by 49 percent in the year to March, a bigger rise than anywhere else."

People often ask whether the emerging global market for mezcal, or tourism for that matter, is a good thing for Oaxaca. Ultimately, the question is misguided: it is difficult to assign causality to any one factor within a market. In some cases, tourism leads to significant increases in industrialization, while in others it results in more discrete and sometimes less profitable sectors, such as craft products in Oaxaca. And even within the market for craft mezcal, not everyone along the value chain stands to gain in equal fashion. These trade-offs also represent the range of choices people make about the scale of what they produce, the manner in which they consume something, and the amount and type of resources that are expended in buying and selling these products. Oaxaca and its mezcal are a small but significant snapshot of the proposition that something made by hand still has an important place in the world, and it has been this book's modest goal to introduce the human into the abstract principles of competitive advantage that underpin the new global economy.

Acknowledgments

My fieldwork in Oaxaca has depended on the generosity of countless people who over the years allowed me to conduct interviews, sit in on community meetings, participate in workshops, and visit their *palenques.* I am deeply grateful to all who openly shared their knowledge of the Oaxacan mezcal industry with me, even though this book only begins to scratch the surface of the complex web of persons, places, and products that make up the world of mezcal and that of agave spirits more generally. The following individuals warrant special mention: Armando Isidro Aquino, Eric Adalid Hernández, Félix Ángeles Arellanes, Graciela Ángeles Carreño, Gabe Bonfanti, Ron Cooper, Susan Coss, Dafne Díaz de la Vega Núñez, Edgar González, Pedro García Vásquez, Elisandro González, Granville Greene, Cris Guzmán Santiago, Julian Gómez, Félix Hernández Monterrosa, Judah Kuper, Miguel Ángel López Vásquez, Erubiel Mota, Hipócrates Nolasco Cancino, Steve Olson, Sandra Ortíz Brena, Israel Pérez Santiago, Ricardo Pico, Reyna Sánchez, Alberto Sánchez López, William Scanlan III, Alvin Starkman, Clayton Szczech, Ulises Torrentera, Gabriela Torres-Mazuera, and Bertha Vásquez. I am grateful, too, to all those who endeavor to tell the story of mezcal through their own professional and personal experiences.

My compadres in San Antonio Arrazola—Catarino Carrillo and Leticia Aragón, my godsons Misael and Max, and their extended family—offered their unwavering support while I was doing fieldwork in Mexico. Thank you for always being my home away from home. Ana Montes and Víctor Ricárdez Weber have been steadfast friends in Oaxaca for decades.

My approach to this book's subject matter has benefited from discussions with numerous friends and colleagues over the years, including Igor Ayora-Diaz, Bill Beezley, Diego Bustos, Alanna Cant, Michael Chibnik, Scott Cook, Jorge Díaz Hernández, Renata Hryciuk, Walter Little, Arthur Murphy, Abraham Nahón, Ramona Pérez, Leighton Peterson, Judith Romero, Clare Sammells, Ron Waterbury, and Bill Wood.

In the past couple of years, I have had the good fortune to travel with and learn from author Naomi Duguid, who is a role model for how to weave together stories about food, people, and geography in a masterful way. Her writing on food cultures around the world captivated me when I was a graduate student and continues to inspire me today.

I have often said that this book, in keeping with Oaxacan tradition, has two *madrinas* (godmothers). Martha Rees, the *madrina de bautizo* (baptism), was an amazing source of support and feedback while this project was in its infancy (and beyond), while Jayne Howell, the *madrina de graduación* (graduation), checked in with me nearly every day as I was in the final throes of writing, cheering me along to the finish line.

At the University of New Mexico (UNM), I am incredibly grateful to my colleagues in the Department of Geography and Environmental Studies for creating a dynamic and supportive home base, and to my colleagues at the Latin American and Iberian Institute (LAII), where I previously served as director of Latin American studies. Thank you to Advance at UNM, in particular to director Julia Fulghum, for providing a quiet and supportive writing space. Colleagues Lynn Beene, Miriam Gay-Antaki, Jayne Howell, Maria Lane, Manuel Montoya, Melinda Morgan, Ian Stewart, and Marygold Walsh-Dilley all read chapter drafts and gave invaluable feedback. I am particularly grateful to Clayton Szczech for closely reading and commenting on multiple chapters.

Research for this project was made possible by the generous support of several grants and institutions. A Field Research Grant from the LAII and a Research Allocations Committee Grant from the UNM College of Arts and Sciences supported initial research in Oaxaca. A Fulbright–García Robles COMEXUS Scholar award provided me with the time and resources to complete my field research, as well as a wonderful cohort of fellow Fulbright scholars, including Tatyana Kleyn, who became a close friend when we lived together in Oaxaca during our respective grant periods. The Centro de Investigaciones y Estudios Superiores en Antropología Social (CIESAS) Unidad Pacífico Sur hosted me as a visiting researcher during my 2015 stay in Oaxaca, and I want to thank Dr. Margarita Dalton Palomo for extending the invitation. The Welte Institute for Oaxacan Studies provided a hospitable workspace and access to otherwise hard-to-find materials while I was in Mexico. Subsequent funding from UNM's Center for Regional Studies allowed me to continue the many conversations begun in Mexico by hosting a group of mezcal, tequila, and sotol industry representatives for a multiday workshop in Albuquerque, New Mexico. Support for this research was also provided by the UNM College of Arts and Sciences Office of Research in the form of a publication subvention.

My editor at the University of Texas Press, Casey Kittrell, was incredibly patient and encouraging through what seemed like a never-ending writing process—thank you for believing that this story was worth telling and that I was the person to tell it. A big thank-you also goes to Christina Vargas and the rest of the staff at the press for making the editorial process as seamless as possible. I am grateful to Ted Fischer and an anonymous reviewer for the press for the encouraging, thoughtful comments they provided, which made the final version of the book undoubtedly stronger.

An earlier version of chapter 3 appeared as "A Taste for Agave: The Politics of Mezcal Connoisseurship," in *Taste, Politics, and Identities in Mexican Food*, published in 2019 by Bloomsbury Academic. I am grateful to editor Steffan Igor Ayora-Diaz for the invitation to contribute to this important volume. UNM doctoral student Joseph Scala created the book's maps and assisted in other invaluable ways.

This book likely would not have been written had it not been for my former UNM colleagues Erin Debenport and Lindsay Smith, who kept me going through the bleakest moment in my career. They, along with numerous UNM graduate students, had the strength and courage to speak out, when others chose to remain silent, at tremendous professional and personal cost.

My friend and colleague Amy Brandzel passed away in May 2023 as I was finishing the first draft of this manuscript. They were always a huge supporter of me and my work, and we had planned to take a long-overdue trip to Oaxaca in March 2020, when the pandemic cruelly foreclosed on that possibility. I regret that they never got to see the place they listened to me talk about during our friendship of fifteen years.

Mary Louise Montoya welcomed me into her family in the way only a mother could, and I could not love her more for it. Tito, Matilde, and Manuel Montoya made our house into a home, and there is nothing I enjoy more than coming home to you at the end of every day. Manuel, your humor, intellect, and love are behind every word written here. Thank you for being you.

Notes

Preface

1. Beezley's vision was realized when an episode of *In the Americas* was filmed on the hop industry of Washington state's Yakima Valley (episode 402). See *In the Americas* (n.d.).

Introduction

1. The owner of Mayordomo, one of the largest makers of *cremas*, told me that they were most popular among women, as well as among people who were largely unfamiliar with mezcal or did not typically like strong alcoholic beverages.
2. *Raicilla* and *bacanora* are technically types of mezcal, as they both derive from agave. *Raicilla* is produced in the southwestern state of Jalisco, and *bacanora* in the northern state of Sonora. Sotol, produced primarily in Chihuahua but also in Durango and Coahuila, is made from a different plant genus (*Dasylirion*) than agave (whose genus is *Agave*), one commonly referred to in English as "Desert Spoon."
3. COMERCAM has gone by the name Consejo Regulador del Mezcal (CRM) at different times, and some people still refer to the entity as such.
4. Judah Kuper, founder of Mezcal Vago, explained to me that these classifications are slippery because some "wild" agaves are now also cultivated or receive some form of human intervention, even when they are found growing in nature (i.e., not in an agricultural setting). For this reason, he said, Mezcal Vago uses the term "rare" for its agaves (pers. comm. 2015).
5. Natural fermentation relies on wild, airborne yeast rather than the addition of industrially produced yeast.
6. In addition, Cooper has legally trademarked other mezcal-related phrases: "Sip it, don't shoot it," "From the heart of the maguey, and the soul of the village," and "Single Village Mezcal."

Chapter 1: Mezcal and Coloniality

1. Translated as "firewater," *aguardiente* is a general term in Spanish for distilled drinks made from a variety of local ingredients, most commonly fermented and distilled sugarcane.
2. This is not to minimize the real risks associated with alcohol consumption, particularly with regard to unregulated products that might not comply with accepted safety standards.
3. The "Old World" in this framework refers not only to Europe but to the entire eastern hemisphere.
4. Tepache is a traditional beverage typically made from pineapple or soured pulque.
5. The modern denomination of origin (DO) guidelines allow for tequila to be produced in other states of Mexico, so it is no longer only produced only in Jalisco.
6. Nueva Galicia was an autonomous kingdom of the Viceroyalty of New Spain. It would later become the present-day states of Aguascalientes, Guanajuato, Colima, Jalisco, Nayarit, and Zacatecas.
7. The company, Beam Suntory, also owns Commemorative, Hornitos, and Tres Generaciones tequila brands.
8. *Rancheras,* mariachi, and corridos share musical roots and subject matter. In comparison to *rancheras,* corridos are generally distinguished for their more elaborate storytelling functions, and mariachi for its larger ensembles.

Chapter 2: Mezcal in the New Craft Imaginary

1. Weber describes disenchantment as a sociological condition (i.e., the retreat of magic and myth from social life through processes of secularization and rationalization). However, the term originates with German philosopher Friedrich Schiller's treatise on modern fragmentation and the role of aesthetics.
2. Zignum is made in Oaxaca by the company Casa Armando Guillermo Prieto.
3. One tequila website notes that "instead of cooking [the agave] first, and then separating the sugars from the fibers, a diffuser extracts the starches (fructans) first, using blasts of high-pressure water as agaves pass by on a conveyer belt. The cooking process happens later, if at all" (Sanschagrin 2017).

Chapter 3: A Taste for Agave

1. The Beverage Testing Institute is an independent, Chicago-based marketing service company for wines, beers, and spirits. Founded in 1981, it also sponsors the World Beer Championship. *Reposado con gusano* refers to a mezcal that is "rested" or aged and whose bottle includes a "worm" (an insect larva found on agave plants—or maguey plants, as agave is often called in Oaxaca and other parts of Mexico).

2. Most "artisanal" mezcal will have a minimum ABV of 45 percent (90 proof), and many register around 55–56 percent. Unlike with tequila, the denomination of origin (DO) for mezcal does not specify that it must be made of a single type of agave. Indeed, learning to appreciate the flavors of different agave varietals is an important aspect of mezcal connoisseurship.
3. "Airport mezcal" is approximately twenty to thirty dollars a bottle in the United States, and even less in Mexico. The artisanal mezcals that are gaining traction in the US market, in contrast, are typically forty dollars and up, with some bottles costing over a hundred dollars.

Chapter 4: Mezcal, Mole, and Oaxaca Tourism

1. Downs more recently launched a restaurant and performance venue in Oaxaca City called Humito Cocina y Foro 8 Temblor.
2. Notably, there are artisanal tequila producers in Jalisco, and some of these have become integrated into the type of microdistillery tourism seen in Oaxaca. However, larger, commercial enterprises still command the lion's share of the tourism sector.
3. These organizers included Graciela Ángeles Carreño from Real Minero, Ulises Torrentera from In Situ, and Marco Ochoa from Mezcaloteca.
4. Class in Mexico, like everywhere else, is shaped by the unique historical, economic, and social factors of its region. The food and beverage preferences of middle- and upper-middle-class Americans do not neatly map onto those of the same classes in Mexico. See Walker (2013).
5. I personally accompanied Ron Cooper of Del Maguey Mezcal, Clayton Szczech of Experience Agave, and Alvin Starkman of Mezcal Educational Tours. Citing the popular *Mezcalistas* blog (see Mezcalistas, n.d.), García Garza (2021) identifies the following as leading mezcal tours and tour guides: Erick Rodríguez (Alma Mezcalera), Clayton Szczech (Experience Agave), Tess Rose Lampert, Ferron Salniker, Bobby Heugel, Darinel Silva, Vinik Jure (Expressions of Mezcal), León Lory, Brooks Bailey, and Anna Bruce (Rambling Spirits), Asis Cortés (Puro Burro), Alvin Starkman (Mezcal Educational Tours), Marco Ochoa (Mezcouting), Luis Nogales (Mezcología), and Omar Alonso (Oaxacking).
6. The issue of who is and is not Indigenous in Oaxaca is complicated and not reducible to their speaking an Indigenous language, although that is one of the most common markers of Indigeneity.

Chapter 5: Valuing Women or Creating Value?

1. Notably, one of Sánchez's female neighbors also made mezcal, but because she was married, the finished product was almost always attributed to her husband, even though struggles with his health often prevented him from partaking in its production.

2. At the time of this writing, Sánchez's mezcal was also being sold internationally under the Rezpiral label (Rezpiral, n.d.).
3. Rios Murrieta is now retired from the company and has since launched a nonalcoholic drink brand called JAS.

Chapter 6: Can Mezcal Save a Village?

1. To date there has been no comprehensive survey that correlates emigration activity with household income among mezcal producers. Demographic information collected by the Mexican census bureau, INEGI, does not isolate economic activity with this degree of specificity.
2. He eventually started producing rum in addition to mezcal. His rum is now commercially available under the brand Dakabend.
3. I use pseudonyms for the employees at this distillery because they are not public figures and have not shared their personal stories as part of developing professional personas related to their mezcal brands.
4. The role of *madrina* is typically associated with Catholic rites such as baptism and first Communion, but it is also common for school-age children in Oaxaca to ask a family friend or relative to be a *madrina* or *padrino* (godfather) for graduation milestones.
5. It is common for children to live with their families until marrying and establishing their own households.
6. As with other states in Mexico, there is a cartel presence in Oaxaca. However, drug trafficking in communities where mezcal is also produced is a topic few have been willing to touch, and with good reason.

Bibliography

Adamson, Glenn. 2013. *The Invention of Craft*. London: Bloomsbury Visual Arts.

AIEDMX. 2015. "La Palenquerita." YouTube video, 30:00, posted October 8, 2015. https://www.youtube.com/watch?v=D3RXbUcOnBM.

Alba, Francisco, and Joseph E. Potter. 1986. "Population and Development in Mexico since 1940: An Interpretation." *Population and Development Review* 12 (1): 47–75.

Alonso, Ana Maria. 2008. "Conforming Disconformity: 'Mestizaje,' Hybridity, and the Aesthetics of Mexican Nationalism." *Cultural Anthropology* 19 (4): 459–490.

Alvarado Juárez, Ana Margarita. 2008. "Migración y pobreza en Oaxaca." *El Cotidiano*, no. 148, 85–94.

Anawalt, Patricia Rieff. 1993. "Rabbits, *Pulque*, and Drunkenness: A Study of Ambivalence in Aztec Society." In *Current Topics in Aztec Studies: Essays in Honor of Dr. H. B. Nicholson*, edited by Alana Cordy-Collins and Douglas Sharon, 17–38. San Diego: San Diego Museum Papers.

Anders, Ferdinand. 1991. *Codex Borbonicus*. 2 vols. Madrid: Sociedad Estatal Quinto Centenario.

Appadurai, Arjun. 1986. *The Social Life of Things: Commodities in Cultural Perspective*. Cambridge: Cambridge University Press.

Appadurai, Arjun. 1996. *Modernity at Large: Cultural Dimensions of Globalization*. Minneapolis: University of Minnesota Press.

Arellanes Meixueiro, Anselmo. 1997. *Mezcal: Elixir de larga vida*. Mexico City: CVS Publicaciones.

Arellano, Gustavo. 2018. "As Oaxaca's Food Scene Booms, Restaurateurs Say Teacher Protests Imperil Business." *The Salt* (blog). National Public Radio, June 26, 2018. https://www.npr.org/sections/thesalt/2018/06/26/621434758.

Arellano-Plaza, Melchor, Jesús Bernardo Paez-Lerma, Nicolás Oscar Soto-Cruz, Manuel R. Kirchmayr, and Anne Gschaedler Mathis. 2022. "Mezcal Production in Mexico: Between Tradition and Commercial Exploitation." *Frontiers in Sustainable Food Systems* 6. https://doi.org/10.3389/fsufs.2022.832532.

Asimov, Eric. 2010. "Mezcal, Tequila's Smoky, Spicy Cousin." *New York Times*, August 16, 2010.

Asimov, Eric. 2020. "With Mezcal, Smoke Is Only Part of the Story." *New York Times*, January 23, 2020.

Ayora-Diaz, Steffan Igor, ed. 2017. *Cooking Technology: Transformations in Culinary Practice in Mexico and Latin America*. New York: Bloomsbury.

Bacon, David. 2013. *The Right to Stay Home: How US Policy Drives Mexican Migration*. Boston: Beacon Press.

Bada, Xóchitl, and Jonathan Fox. 2022. "Persistent Rurality in Mexico and 'the Right to Stay Home.'" *Journal of Peasant Studies* 49 (1): 29–53.

Ballatori, Maureen. 2022. "How to Build a Premium Artisanal Brand." *Forbes*, July 6, 2022. https://www.forbes.com/sites/forbesbusinesscouncil/2022/07/06/how-to-build-a-premium-artisanal-brand.

Barbieri, Jonathan. n.d. "Painter, Writer, Producer, Distiller." Accessed April 15, 2024. https://en.jonathanbarbieri.com/about.

Bartra, Eli. 2011. *Women in Mexican Folk Art: Of Promises, Betrayals, Monsters and Celebrities*. Cardiff: University of Wales Press.

Baskes, Jeremy. 2000. *Indians, Merchants, and Markets: A Reinterpretation of the* Repartimiento *and Spanish-Indian Economic Relations in Colonial Oaxaca, 1750–1821*. Stanford, CA: Stanford University Press.

Beck, Ulrich, and Natan Sznaider. 2010. "Unpacking Cosmopolitanism for the Social Sciences: A Research Agenda." *British Journal of Sociology* 61 (s1): 381–403.

Belasco, Warren J. 2006. *Appetite for Change: How the Counterculture Took on the Food Industry*. 2nd ed. Ithaca, NY: Cornell University Press.

Bell, David, and Gill Valentine. 1997. *Consuming Geographies: We Are Where We Eat*. New York: Routledge.

Bell, Emma, M. Tina Dacin, and Maria Laura Toraldo. 2021. "Craft Imaginaries—Past, Present and Future." *Organization Theory* 2 (1). https://doi.org/10.1177/2631787721991141.

Berger, Dina. 2006. *The Development of Mexico's Tourism Industry: Pyramids by Day, Martinis by Night*. New York: Palgrave Macmillan.

Besky, Sarah. 2013. *The Darjeeling Distinction: Labor and Justice on Fair-Trade Tea Plantations in India*. Berkeley: University of California Press.

Black, Rachel E. 2021. *Cheffes de Cuisine: Women and Work in the Professional French Kitchen*. Champaign: University of Illinois Press.

Black, Rachel E., and Robert C. Ulin, eds. 2013. *Wine and Culture: Vineyard to Glass*. New York: Bloomsbury.

Boltanski, Luc, and Arnaud Esquerre. 2020. *Enrichment: A Critique of Commodities*. Translated by Catherine Porter. Cambridge: Polity Press.

Boone, Elizabeth Hill. 1983. *The Codex Magliabechiano and the Lost Prototype of the Magliabechiano Group*. 2 vols. Berkeley: University of California Press.

Bourdieu, Pierre. 1984. *Distinction: A Social Critique of the Judgement of Taste.* Translated by Richard Nice. Cambridge: Harvard University Press.

Bowen, Sarah. 2015. *Divided Spirits: Tequila, Mezcal, and the Politics of Production.* Berkeley: University of California Press.

Bowen, Sarah, and Ana Valenzuela-Zapata. 2009. "Geographical Indications, *terroir*, and Socioeconomic and Ecological Sustainability: The Case of Tequila." *Journal of Rural Studies* 25 (1): 108–119.

Brandes, Stanley H. 2002. *Staying Sober in Mexico City*. Austin: University of Texas Press.

Brewers Association. n.d. "National Beer Sales & Production Data." Accessed May 23, 2023. https://www.brewersassociation.org/statistics-and-data/national-beer-stats.

Bruce, Anna. 2024. "Drought: The Water Reality in Oaxaca." *Mezcalistas* (blog). March 20, 2024. https://www.mezcalistas.com/drought.

Brulotte, Ronda L. 2012. *Between Art and Artifact: Archaeological Replicas and Cultural Production in Oaxaca, Mexico*. Austin: University of Texas Press.

Brulotte, Ronda L. 2017. "Alcohol and Ambivalence in Mexico and the Americas." *Latin American Research Review* 52 (5): 910–915.

Brulotte, Ronda L. 2019. "A Taste for Agave: The Politics of Mezcal Connoisseurship." In *Taste, Politics, and Identities in Mexican Food*, edited by Steffan Igor Ayora-Diaz, 83–99. London: Bloomsbury.

Brulotte, Ronda L., and M. J. R. Montoya. 2019. "Defining Craft: Hermeneutics and Economy." In *A Cultural Economic Analysis of Craft*, edited by Anna Mignosa and Priyatej Kotipalli, 15–23. New York: Palgrave Macmillan.

Bruman, Henry J. 2000. *Alcohol in Ancient Mexico*. Salt Lake City: University of Utah Press.

Cailleba, Patrice, and Herbert Casteran. 2010. "Do Ethical Values Work? A Quantitative Study of the Impact of Fair Trade Coffee on Consumer Behavior." *Journal of Business Ethics* 97:613–624.

Candlin, Christopher N., and Yon Maley. 1997. "Intertextuality and Interdiscursivity in the Discourse of Alternative Dispute Resolution." In *The Construction of Professional Discourse*, edited by Britt-Louise Gunnarsson, Per Linell, and Bengt Nordberg, 201–222. London: Longman.

Cant, Alanna. 2019. *The Value of Aesthetics: Oaxacan Woodcarvers in Global Economies of Culture*. Austin: University of Texas Press.

Cappeliez, Sarah, and Josée Johnston. 2013. "From Meat and Potatoes to 'Real-Deal' Rotis: Exploring Everyday Culinary Cosmopolitanism." *Poetics* 41 (5): 433–455.

Carruthers, Nicola. 2020. "Bacardi 'Not Proud' of Plume and Petal Marketing." *Spirits Business*, July 22, 2020. https://www.thespiritsbusiness.com/2020/07/bacardi.

Cave, Damien. 2011. "Better Lives for Mexicans Cut Allure of Going North." *New York Times*, July 6, 2013.

Chabrol, Didier, and José Muchnik. 2011. "Consumer Skills Contribute to Maintaining and Diffusing Heritage Food Products." *Anthropology of Food* 8. https://doi.org/10.4000/aof.6847.

Chance, John K. 1978. *Race and Class in Colonial Oaxaca*. Stanford, CA: Stanford University Press.

Chance, John K., and William B. Taylor. 1977. "Estate and Class in a Colonial City: Oaxaca in 1792." *Comparative Studies in Society and History* 19 (4): 454–487.

Chassen-López, Francie. 2014. "The Traje de Tehuana as National Icon: Gender, Ethnicity, and Fashion in Mexico." *Americas* 71 (2): 281–314.

Chasteen, John Charles. 2016. *Born in Blood and Fire: A Concise History of Latin America*. 4th ed. New York: W. W. Norton.

Chibnik, Michael. 2003. *Crafting Tradition: The Making and Marketing of Oaxacan Wood Carvings*. Austin: University of Texas Press.

Coe, Sophie D. 1994. *America's First Cuisines*. Austin: University of Texas Press.

Coffey, Mary K. 2018. "Great Masters of Mexican Folk Art in Los Angeles: Transnational Exhibition, Diasporic Emplacement, and the Expedient Politics of Display." *Cultural Studies* 32 (2): 194–222.

Cohen, Jeffrey H. 1999. *Community and Cooperation: Economy and Society in Oaxaca*. Austin: University of Texas Press.

Cohen, Jeffrey H. 2004. *The Culture of Migration in Southern Mexico*. Austin: University of Texas Press.

Colunga-García Marín, Patricia, Alfonso Larqué Saavedra, Luis E. Eguiarte, and Daniel Zizumbo Villareal, eds. 2007. *En lo ancestral hay futuro: del tequila, los mezcales y otros agaves*. Mexico City: Impresora y Encuadernadora Progreso.

Colwell, Chip. 2022. "A Palimpsest Theory of Objects." *Current Anthropology* 63 (2): 129–157.

COMERCAM. 2024. "Informe Estadístico 2024." Accessed May 5, 2024. https://comercam-dom.org.mx/estadisticas.

COMERCAM (Mexican Regulatory Council for Mezcal Quality). n.d. Home page. Accessed April 15, 2024. https://comercam-dom.org.mx.

Cook, Ian. 2004. "Follow the Thing: Papaya." *Antipode* 36 (4): 642–664.

Cook, Scott. 2014. *Land, Livelihood, and Civility in Southern Mexico: Oaxaca Valley Communities in History*. Austin: University of Texas Press.

Cook, Scott, and Martin Diskin, eds. 1975. *Markets in Oaxaca*. Austin: University of Texas Press.

Cooper, Ron, and Chantal Martineau. 2018. *Finding Mezcal: A Journey into the Liquid Soul of Mexico, with 40 Cocktails*. Berkeley, CA: Ten Speed Press.

Coss, Susan. 2022. "Mezcal Is Mainstream, So Now What?" *Mezcalistas* (blog). December 29, 2022. https://www.mezcalistas.com/mezcal-is-mainstream.

Creo Chocolate. n.d. "The Creo Story." Accessed April 15, 2024. https://creochocolate.com/pages/about-us.

Dare, Rebecca, Håkan Jönsson, and Hans Knutsson. 2013. "Adding Value in Food Production." In *Food Industry*, edited by Innocenzo Muzzalupo. London: IntechOpen. https://www.doi.org/10.5772/53174.

Data México. n.d. "Oaxaca." Accessed April 2, 2023. https://www.economia.gob.mx/datamexico/en/profile/geo/oaxaca-oa#economy.

Davidson, Joanna. 2015. *Sacred Rice: An Ethnography of Identity, Environment, and Development in Rural West Africa*. Oxford: Oxford University Press.

De Barrios, Virginia B. 2002. *A Guide to Tequila, Mezcal and Pulque*. Mexico City: Editorial Minutiae Mexicana.

De Gortari, Yuri, and Edmundo Escamilla. 2009. *Mezcal, nuestra esencia*. Mexico City: Ambar Diseño.

Deleuze, Gilles, and Félix Guattari. 2009. *Anti-Oedipus: Capitalism and Schizophrenia*. New York: Penguin Books.

Diaz-Bone, Rainer. 2023. "An Interview with Luc Boltanski and Arnaud Esquerre on *Enrichment: A Critique of Commodities*." *Theory, Culture & Society* 40 (7–8): 17–32.

Di Giovine, Michael A. 2008. *The Heritage-scape: UNESCO, World Heritage, and Tourism*. Lanham, MD: Lexington Books.

Dingwall, Kate. 2021. "In the U.S., Craft Spirits Are Outpacing Major Brands." *Forbes*, November 27, 2021. https://www.forbes.com/sites/katedingwall/2021/11/27/in-the-us-craft-spirits-are-outpacing-major-brands.

Distiller. n.d. "Koch el Mezcal Ensemble." Accessed April 15, 2024. https://distiller.com/spirits/koch-el-mezcal-ensemble.

Earle, Rebecca. 2008. "Algunos pensamientos sobre 'El indio borracho' en el imaginario criollo." *Revista de Estudios Sociales* 29:18–27.

Eber, Christine. 2000. *Women and Alcohol in a Highland Maya Town: Water of Hope, Water of Sorrow*. Rev. ed. Austin: University of Texas Press.

Economist. 2019. "Can Tourism Boost One of Mexico's Poorest States?" July 25, 2019.

Eden, Lorraine, and Stewart R. Miller. 2004. "Distance Matters: Liability of Foreignness, Institutional Distance and Ownership Strategy." In *Theories of the Multinational Enterprise: Diversity, Complexity and Relevance*, edited by Michael A. Hitt and Joseph L. C. Cheng, 187–221. Somerville, MA: Emerald.

Eisenstein, Hester. 2009. *Feminism Seduced: How Global Elites Use Women's Labor and Ideas to Exploit the World*. Boulder, CO: Paradigm.

Eldridge, Alison. "Etsy." *Britannica Money*. Updated March 30, 2024. https://www.britannica.com/money/Etsy.

Errington, Shelly. 1998. *The Death of Authentic Primitive Art: And Other Tales of Progress*. Berkeley: University of California Press.

Escalante, Adelfo, David R López Soto, Judith E. Velázquez Gutiérrez, Martha Giles-Gómez, Francisco Bolívar, and Agustín López-Munguía. 2016. "*Pulque*, a Traditional Mexican Alcoholic Fermented Beverage: Historical, Microbiological, and Technical Aspects." *Frontiers in Microbiology* 7. https://www.doi.org/10.3389/fmicb.2016.01026.

Espiritu. n.d. Home page. Accessed April 15, 2024. https://espiritu.com.

Experience Agave. n.d. "Oaxaca Mezcal Pechuga Camp." Accessed April 15, 2024. https://www.experienceagave.com/experience-mezcal-tours/mezcal-pechuga-camp.

Farber, David. 2016. "Self-Invention in the Realm of Production: Craft, Beauty, and Community in the American Counterculture, 1964–1978." *Pacific Historical Review* 85 (3): 408–442.

Feinberg, Benjamin. 2003. *The Devil's Book of Culture: History, Mushrooms, and Caves in Southern Mexico*. Austin: University of Texas Press.

Fernández de Calderón, Cándida, and Alberto Sarmiento. 2021. *Great Masters of Mexican Folk Art: From the Collection of Fomento Cultural Banamex*. New York: Harry N. Abrams.

Fischer, Edward F. 2022. *Making Better Coffee: How Maya Farmers and Third Wave Tastemakers Create Value*. Oakland: University of California Press.

Fischer, Edward F., and Peter Benson. 2006. *Broccoli and Desire: Global Connections and Maya Struggles in Postwar Guatemala*. Stanford, CA: Stanford University Press.

Flash, Emma. 2021. "El imbatible equipo mezcalero de Tlacotitlanapa." *Destilados Campesinos de México* (blog). May 15, 2021. http://www.destiladoscampesinos.com/2021/05/15/el.

Fox, Jonathan, and Gaspar Rivera-Salgado, eds. 2004. *Indigenous Mexican Migrants in the United States*. San Diego, CA: Center for US-Mexican Studies.

Friedman, Ann. 2013. "How Do You Change a Bro-Dominated Culture?" *New York Magazine*, September 12, 2013.

Gálvez, Alyshia. 2018. *Eating NAFTA: Trade, Food Policies, and the Destruction of Mexico*. Berkeley: University of California Press.

Gálvez, Alyshia. 2021. "Paqueteros and Paqueteras: Humanizing a Dehumanized Food System." *Gastronomica* 21 (1): 27–37.

García Canclini, Néstor. 1995. *Hybrid Cultures: Strategies for Entering and Leaving Modernity*. Translated by Christopher L. Chiappari and Silvia L. López. Minneapolis: University of Minnesota Press.

García Canclini, Néstor. 2010. *Transforming Modernity: Popular Culture in Mexico*. Austin: University of Texas Press.

García Garza, Domingo. 2019. *Mezcal: un espirituoso artesanal de clase mundial*. Oaxaca, Mexico: 1450 Ediciones.

García Garza, Domingo. 2021. "Las visitas guiadas a microdestilerías en México: Algunas observaciones etnográficas sobre el turismo mezcalero." *Cultura y Representaciones Sociales* 16 (31): 63–99.

García Garza, Domingo. 2022. *La revolución mezcalera: Los destilados de agave y la invención del mezcal tradicional*. Zamora, Mexico: El Colegio de Michoacán.

Garland, Carina. 2008. "Curious Appetites: Food, Desire, Gender and Subjectivity in Lewis Carroll's Alice Texts." *Lion and the Unicorn* 32 (1): 22–39.

Gaudin, Yannick, Ramón Padilla Pérez, and Isidro Soloaga. 2024. *New Methods to Define and Measure Rurality in Latin America and Their Impact on Public Policies: The Cases of Mexico and Panama*. Rome: International Fund for Agricultural Development.

Gaytán, Marie Sarita. 2013. "Drinking Difference: Race, Consumption, and Alcohol Prohibition in Mexico and the United States." *Ethnicities* 14 (3): 436–457.

Gaytán, Marie Sarita. 2014. *¡Tequila! Distilling the Spirit of Mexico*. Stanford, CA: Stanford University Press.

Gaytán, Marie Sarita. 2018. "The Perils of Protection and the Promise of Authenticity: Tequila, Mezcal, and the Case of NOM 186." *Journal of Rural Studies* 58:103–111.

Gaytán, Marie Sarita. 2019. "Extending Authenticity: Going Corporate in a Craft Market." *Poetics* 77. https://doi.org/10.1016/j.poetic.2019.101380.

Ghemawat, Pankaj. 2007. *Redefining Global Strategy: Crossing Borders in a World Where Differences Still Matter*. Boston: Harvard Business School Press.

Gimmel, Atalie. 2021. "How This Woman-Made Mezcal Combines Mexican Tradition and Modernity." Photography by Mallika Vora. *Vogue*, September 24, 2021. https://www.vogue.com/article/dona-vega-mezcal-la-curva-santiago-matatlan.

Ginzberg, Eitan. 2020. "Genocide and the Hispanic-American Dilemma." *Genocide Studies and Prevention* (14) 2: 122–152.

Goodyear, Dana. 2016. "Mezcal Sunrise: Searching for the Ultimate Artisanal Distillate." *New Yorker*, March 28, 2016.

Gravel, Nathalie. 2007. "Mexican Smallholders Adrift: The Urgent Need for a New Social Contract in Rural Mexico." *Journal of Latin American Geography* 6 (2): 77–98.

Greene, Granville E. 2017. *The Mezcal Rush: Explorations in Agave Country*. Berkeley, CA: Counterpoint.

Hart, John Mason. 2006. *Empire and Revolution: The Americans in Mexico since the Civil War*. Berkeley: University of California Press.

Hartman, Eviana. 2016. "Lykke Li Debuts Her New Band—And Soon-to-Launch Mezcal Brand—With a Hollywood House Party." *Vogue*, April 22, 2016. https://www.vogue.com/article/lykke-li-yola-mezcal-hollywood-party.

Harvey, David C. 2008. "The History of Heritage." In *The Routledge Research Companion to Heritage and Identity*, edited by Peter Howard and Brian Graham, 19–36. New York: Routledge.

Heirloom Cacao. n.d. Home page. Accessed April 15, 2024. https://www.hcpcacao.org.

Heldke, Lisa. 2003. *Exotic Appetites: Ruminations of a Food Adventurer*. New York: Routledge.

Herz, Julia. 2014. "The Roots of American Craft Brewing." *Craft Beer Muses* (blog). May 15, 2014. https://www.craftbeer.com/craft-beer-muses/the-roots-of-american-craft-brewing.

Howell, Jayne. 2023. *Women Teachers of Rural Oaxaca: Agency and Empowerment*. Lanham, MD: Lexington Books.

Hryciuk, Renata E. 2019. "Alquimista de los Sabores: Gastronomic Heritage, Gender, and the Tourist Imaginary in Mexico." *Revista del CESLA: International Latin American Studies Review* 24:75–100.

Huerta Rosas, Rogelio, and Rogelio Luna Zamora. 2015. "Los caminos del mezcal y el tequila." In *Agua de las verdes matas: Tequila y mezcal*, edited by José Luis Vera Cortés and Rodolfo Fernández, 43–66. Mexico City: Artes de Mexico y del Mundo.

In the Americas. n.d. Series page. Accessed April 15, 2024. https://intheamericas.org.

Irwin, Robert McKee, and Maricruz Castro Ricalde. 2013. *Global Mexican Cinema: Its Golden Age*. New York: Bloomsbury.

Jackson, Harvey H., III. 2013. *The Rise and Decline of the Redneck Riviera: An Insider's History of the Florida-Alabama Coast*. Athens: University of Georgia Press.

Janzen, Emma. 2017. *Mezcal: The History, Craft and Cocktails of the World's Ultimate Artisanal Spirit*. Minneapolis, MN: Voyageur Press.

Japhe, Brad. 2018. "Forget Mezcal, Sotol Is Mexico's Hottest New Spirit." *Forbes*, July 26, 2018. https://www.forbes.com/sites/bradjaphe/2018/07/26/forget-mezcal-sotol-is-mexicos-hottest-new-spirit.

Japhe, Brad. 2022. "This Mexico Hot Spot Was Just Named the Best City in the World by T+L Readers—Here's How to Plan the Perfect Trip." *Travel and Leisure*, July 17, 2022. https://www.travelandleisureasia.com/in/destinations/this-mexico-hot-spot-was-named-the-best-city-in-the-world.

Joassart-Marcelli, Pascale, and Fernando J. Bosco, eds. 2017. *Food and Place: A Critical Exploration*. New York: Rowman and Littlefield.

Johnston, Josée, and Shyon Baumann. 2014. *Foodies: Democracy and Distinction in the Gourmet Foodscape*. 2nd ed. New York: Routledge.

Jolly, Jennifer. 2018. *Creating Pátzcuaro, Creating Mexico: Art, Tourism, and Nation Building under Lázaro Cárdenas*. Austin: University of Texas Press.

José Cuervo Express. n.d. Accessed April 15, 2024. http://www.josecuervoexpress.com.

Joseph, Gilbert M., Anne Rubenstein, and Eric Zolov, eds. 2001. *Fragments of a Golden Age: The Politics of Culture in Mexico since 1940*. Durham, NC: Duke University Press.

Kearney, Michael. 1995a. "The Effects of Transnational Culture, Economy, and Migration on Mixtec Identity in Oaxacalifornia." In *The Bubbling Cauldron: Race, Ethnicity, and the Urban Crisis*, edited by Michael Peter Smith and Joe R. Feagin, 226–243. Minneapolis: University of Minnesota Press.

Kearney, Michael. 1995b. "The Local and the Global: The Anthropology of Globalization and Transnationalism." *Annual Review of Anthropology* 24:547–565.

Kearney, Michael. 1996. *Reconceptualizing the Peasantry: Anthropology in Global Perspective*. Boulder, CO: Westview Press.

Kennedy, Diana. 1972. *The Cuisines of Mexico*. New York: Harper and Row.

Kennedy, Diana. 2008. *Oaxaca al gusto: El mundo infinito de su gastronomía*. San Pedro Garza García, Mexico: Plenus.

Kennedy, Diana. 2010. *Oaxaca al gusto: An Infinite Gastronomy*. Austin: University of Texas Press.

Klamer, Arjo. 1996. *The Value of Culture: On the Relationship between Economics and Arts*. Amsterdam: University of Amsterdam Press.

Knight, Alan. 1990. "Racism, Revolution, and Indigenismo: Mexico, 1910–1940." In *The Idea of Race in Latin America, 1870–1940*, edited by Richard Graham, 71–113. Austin: University of Texas Press.

Knight, Alan. 1991. "Land and Society in Revolutionary Mexico: The Destruction of the Great Haciendas." *Mexican Studies/Estudios Mexicanos* 7 (1): 73–104.

Kopytoff, Igor. 1986. "The Cultural Biography of Things: Commoditization as a Process." In *The Social Life of Things: Commodities in Cultural Perspective*, edited by Arjun Appadurai, 64–91. Cambridge: Cambridge University Press.

Lampert, Tess Rose. 2023. *The Essential Tequila & Mezcal Companion: How to Select, Collect and Savor Agave Sprits*. New York: Union Square.

La Niña del Mezcal. n.d. Instagram page (@laninadelmezcal). Accessed April 15, 2024. https://www.instagram.com/laninadelmezcal.

Laudan, Rachel. 2015. *Cuisine and Empire: Cooking in World History*. Berkeley: University of California Press.

Laudan, Rachel, and Jeffrey M. Pilcher. 1999. "Chiles, Chocolate, and Race in New Spain: Glancing Backward to Spain or Looking Forward to Mexico?" *Eighteenth-Century Life* 23 (2): 59–70.

Lauri, Johanna, and Hanna Bäckström. 2019. "Coffee by Women: The 'Duty of Ethical Enjoyment.'" *Cultural Studies* 33 (5): 866–887.

Lawson, Robert. 2020. "Language and Masculinities: History, Development, and Future." *Annual Review of Linguistics* 6:409–434.

Lemmon, Gayle Tzemach. 2012. "Entrepreneurship in Postconflict Zones." Working paper, Council on Foreign Relations, New York.

Lévi-Strauss, Claude. 1962. *Le totémisme aujourd'hui*. Paris: Presses universitaires de France.

Lira, María G., James P. Robson, and Daniel J. Klooster. 2022. "Commons, Global Markets and Small-Scale Family Enterprises: The Case of Mezcal Production in Oaxaca, Mexico." *Agriculture and Human Values* 39:937–952.

Littaye, Alexandra Z. 2016. "The Multifunctionality of Heritage Food: The Example of Pinole, a Mexican Sweet." *Geoforum* 76:11–19.

Long, Lucy M. 2004. Introduction to *Culinary Tourism*, edited by Lucy M. Long, 1–19. Louisville: University of Kentucky Press.

López, Rick A. 2010. *Crafting Mexico: Intellectuals, Artisans, and the State after the Revolution*. Durham, NC: Duke University Press.

Lowry, Malcolm. 1947. *Under the Volcano*. New York: Reynal and Hitchcock.

MacCannell, Dean. (1976) 1999. *The Tourist: A New Theory of the Leisure Class.* Berkeley: University of California Press.

Manning, Paul. 2012. *Semiotics of Drink and Drinking.* New York: Continuum International.

Marichal Salinas, Carlos. 2018. "Mexican Cochineal, Local Technologies and the Rise of Global Trade from the Sixteenth to the Nineteenth Centuries." In *Global History and New Polycentric Approaches,* edited by Manuel Perez Garcia and Lucio de Sousa, 255–273. Singapore: Palgrave Macmillan.

Martineau, Chantal. 2015a. *How Gringos Stole Tequila: The Modern Age of Mexico's Most Traditional Spirit.* Chicago: Chicago Review Press.

Martineau, Chantal. 2015b. "Move Over, Tequila: Why Artisanal Mezcal Is on the Rise." *Vogue,* August 20, 2015. https://www.vogue.com/article/mezcal-ancient-artisanal-cocktail-tequila.

Martínez, Oscar J. 2016. *Mexico's Uneven Development: The Geographical and Historical Context of Inequality.* New York: Routledge.

Matta, Raúl. 2019. "Mexico's Ethnic Culinary Heritage and *cocineras tradicionales* (Traditional Female Cooks)." *Food and Foodways* 27 (3): 211–231.

McClain, Joe. 2018. "Tequila, a Great Contribution for Tourism in Mexico." *Tourism Review News,* December 10, 2018. https://www.tourism-review.com/tequila-has-great-contribution-for-tourism-news10866.

McEvoy, John P. 2013. "What Does Mezcal Taste Like?" *Mezcal PhD* (blog). September 26, 2013. https://mezcalphd.com/2013/09/what.

McEvoy, John P. 2014. *Holy Smoke! It's Mezcal! A Complete Guide from Agave to Zapotec.* New York: Mezcal PhD.

McEvoy, John P. 2018. "Tequila vs. Mezcal." *Mezcal PhD* (blog). November 24, 2018. https://mezcalphd.com/2018/11/tequila.

McGehee, Nancy Gard. 2014. "Volunteer Tourism: Evolution, Issues and Futures." *Journal of Sustainable Tourism* 22 (6): 847–854.

McGovern, Patrick E., Fabian H. Toro, Gretchen R. Hall, Theodore Davidson, Katharine Prokop Prigge, George Preti, W. Christian Petersen, and Mike Szelewski. 2019. "Pre-Hispanic Distillation? A Biomolecular Archaeological Investigation." *Open Access Journal of Archaeology and Anthropology* 1 (2). https://www.doi.org/10.33552/OAJAA.2019.01.000509.

McRobbie, Angela. 2009. *The Aftermath of Feminism: Gender, Culture and Social Change.* London: Sage.

Mercado López, Eugenio. 2022. "Artisans and Crafts in Postrevolutionary Mexico." In *Performing Craft in Mexico: Artisans, Aesthetics, and the Power of Translation,* edited by Michele Avis Feder-Nadoff, 41–60. Lanham, MD: Lexington Books.

México Desconocido. n.d. "Pueblos Mágicos." Accessed April 15, 2024. https://pueblosmagicos.mexicodesconocido.com.mx.

Mezcalistas. n.d. Home page. Accessed April 15, 2024. https://www.mezcalistas.com.

Mezcaloteca. n.d. "About Us." Accessed April 15, 2024. https://mezcaloteca.com/en/pages/nosotros.

Mezcal Reviews. n.d.a. "Del Maguey Chichicapa." Accessed April 15, 2024. https://www.mezcalreviews.com/mezcal/del-maguey-chichicapa.

Mezcal Reviews. n.d.b. "Del Maguey Wild Papalome." Accessed May 20, 2024. https://www.mezcalreviews.com/mezcal/del-maguey-wild-papalome.

Mezcal Vago. n.d. "The Story." Accessed April 15, 2024. https://mezcalvago.com/the-story.

Millán Vázquez de la Torre, Genoveva, José Caridad y Ocerín, Juan Manuel Arjona Fuentes, and Luis Amador Hidalgo. 2014. "Tequila Tourism as a Factor of Development: A Strategic Vision in Mexico." *Tourism and Hospitality Management* 20 (1): 137–149.

Mintz, Sidney W. 1985. *Sweetness and Power: The Place of Sugar in Modern History.* New York: Viking Penguin.

Mitchell, Tim. 2004. *Intoxicated Identities: Alcohol's Power in Mexican History and Culture.* New York: Routledge.

Mostafanezhad, Mary. 2016. *Volunteer Tourism: Popular Humanitarianism in Neoliberal Times.* New York: Routledge.

Murphy, Arthur D., and Alex Stepick. 1991. *Social Inequality in Oaxaca: A History of Resistance and Change.* Philadelphia: Temple University Press.

Nabhan, Gary Paul, and David Suro Piñera. 2023. *Agave Spirits: The Past, Present, and Future of Mezcals.* New York: W. W. Norton.

Nahón, Abraham. 2020. *Imágenes en Oaxaca: Arte, política y memoria.* Oaxaca, Mexico: Universidad Autónoma Benito Juárez de Oaxaca.

Nájera Ramírez, Olga. 1989. "Social and Political Dimensions of Folklorico Dance: The Binational Dialectic of Residual and Emergent Culture." *Western Folklore* 48 (1): 15–32.

Newman, Kara. 2020. "What Do Women Drink?" *Wine Enthusiast,* October 12, 2020. https://www.wineenthusiast.com/culture/spirits/women-spirits-gender-marketing.

Novelo, Victoria. 1976. *Artesanías y capitalismo en México.* Mexico City: Instituto Nacional de Antropología e Historia.

NPR (National Public Radio). 2004. "Mexican Town Relies on Mezcal to Stem Migration." *All Things Considered,* April 21, 2004. https://www.npr.org/2004/04/21/1846265.

NPR (National Public Radio). 2014. "Can Mezcal Save a Village?" *Planet Money,* January 24, 2014. https://www.npr.org/sections/money/2014/01/24/265708532.

Nunn, Nathan, and Nancy Qian. 2010. "The Columbian Exchange: A History of Disease, Food, and Ideas." *Journal of Economic Perspectives* 24 (2): 163–188.

Oaxaca. 2019. "Centro Gastronómico Oaxaca (Real Alhóndiga)." Proposal, April 2019. https://www.oaxaca.gob.mx/sectur/wp-content/uploads/sites/65/2020/12/8.-Propuesta-Centro-Gastronomico-ok.pdf.

Oaxaca Travel. n.d. "Rutas Oaxaca." Accessed April 15, 2024. http://www.oaxaca.travel/index.php/es/rutas-oaxaca.

Orozco, José. 2014. "Tequila Sauza and the Redemption of Mexico's Vital Fluids,

1873–1970." In *Alcohol in Latin America: A Social and Cultural History*, edited by Gretchen Pierce and Áurea Toxqui, 185–209. Tucson: University of Arizona Press.

Pansters, Wil G. 2018. "Drug Trafficking, the Informal Order, and *caciques*: Reflections on the Crime-Governance Nexus in Mexico." *Global Crime* 19 (3–4): 315–338.

Pardo Nuñez, Joaliné, and Graciela Ángeles Carreño. 2021. "Prólogo." In *Miradas femeninas desde el mezcal*, 5–8. Guadalajara: Centro de Investigación y Asistencia en Tecnología y Diseño del Estado de Jalisco.

Parsons, Jeffrey R., and Mary H. Parsons. 1990. *Maguey Utilization in Highland Central Mexico: An Archaeological Ethnography*. Ann Arbor: University of Michigan Press.

Paxson, Heather. 2012. *The Life of Cheese: Crafting Food and Value in America*. Oakland: University of California Press.

Pérez, Ramona L. 2019. "The Taste of Oaxaca: It's to Die for!" In *Taste, Politics, and Identities in Mexican Food*, edited by Steffan Igor Ayora-Diaz, 147–159. London: Bloomsbury.

Picard, David, Catarina Nascimento Moreira, and Tristan Loloum. 2018. "Wine Magic: Consumer Culture, Tourism, and Terroir." *Journal of Anthropological Research* 74 (4): 526–540.

Pierce, Gretchen, and Áurea Toxqui, eds. 2014. *Alcohol in Latin America: A Social and Cultural History*. Tucson: University of Arizona Press.

Pilcher, Jeffrey M. 1998. *¡Que vivan los tamales! Food and the Making of Mexican Identity*. Albuquerque: University of New Mexico Press.

Pilcher, Jeffrey M. 2010. "José Cuervo and the Gentrified Worm: Food, Drink, and the Touristic Consumption of Mexico." In *Holiday in Mexico: Critical Reflections on Tourism and Tourist Encounters*, edited by Dina Berger and Andrew Grant Wood, 221–240. Durham, NC: Duke University Press.

Poister, John J. 1999. *The New American Bartender's Guide*. 3rd ed. New York: Signet.

Polites, Jared. 2020. "Why Artisans Will Be Powerful in the New Economy." *Entrepreneur*, August 26, 2020. https://www.entrepreneur.com/leadership/why-artisans-will-be-powerful-in-the-new-economy/354514.

Rajak, Dinah. 2011. *In Good Company: An Anatomy of Corporate Social Responsibility*. Stanford, CA: Stanford University Press.

Ramírez Rodríguez, Rodolfo. 2018. *La querella por el pulque: Auge y ocaso de una industria mexicana, 1890–1930*. Zamora, Mexico: El Colegio de Michoacán.

Rezpiral. n.d. Home page. Accessed May 24, 2024. https://rezpiral.com.

Robson, James P., Dan Klooster, and Jorge Hernández-Díaz, eds. 2019. *Communities Surviving Migration: Village Governance, Environment and Cultural Survival in Indigenous Mexico*. New York: Routledge.

Rodríguez, Óscar. 2014. "Ruta del Mezcal en Oaxaca está 'en el limbo.'" *Milenio*,

June 1, 2014. https://www.milenio.com/estados/ruta-del-mezcal-en-oaxaca-esta-en-el-limbo.

Rodríguez, Óscar. 2015. "Adela, la niña mezcalera de Oaxaca." *Milenio*, March 15, 2015. https://www.milenio.com/estados/adela-la-nina-mezcalera-de-oaxaca.

Roseberry, William. 1996. "The Rise of Yuppie Coffees and the Reimagination of Class in the United States." *American Anthropologist* 98 (4): 762–775.

Rubenstein, Grace. 2015. "Here Are Three Women Blazing a Trail in the Red-Hot Mezcal Industry." *World*, October 29, 2015. https://theworld.org/stories/2015/10/29/here-are-three-women-blazing-trail-red-hot-mezcal-industry.

Salazar, Noel B., and Nelson H. H. Graburn, eds. 2014. *Tourism Imaginaries: Anthropological Approaches*. New York: Berghahn Books.

Sánchez López, Alberto. 2005. *Oaxaca, tierra de maguey y mezcal*. Oaxaca, Mexico: Comercializadora Oaxaqueña del Centro.

Sánchez Prado, Ignacio M. 2020. "Diana Kennedy, Rick Bayless and the Imagination of 'Authentic' Mexican Food." *Bulletin of Spanish Studies* 97 (4): 567–592.

Sandoval-Cervantes, Iván. 2022. *Oaxaca in Motion: An Ethnography of Internal, Transnational, and Return Migration*. Austin: University of Texas Press.

Sanschagrin, Grover. 2017. "Putting Diffuser-Made Tequilas to the Blind Taste Test." *Taste Tequila* (blog). February 15, 2017. https://tastetequila.com/2017/putting.

Scardaville, Michael C. 1980. "Alcohol Abuse and Tavern Reform in Late Colonial Mexico City." *Hispanic American Historical Review* 60 (4): 643–671.

Schechter, Alex. 2021. "This New Oaxaca Hotel Is a Mezcal Lover's Dream." *Vogue*, July 23, 2021. https://www.vogue.com/article/casa-silencio-new-oaxaca-hotel-mezcal.

Schnepel, Ellen M. 2002. "Chocolate: From Bean to Bar." *Gastronomica* 2 (4): 98–100.

SECTUR (Secretaría de Turismo). n.d. *Ruta gastronómica los mil sabores del mole: Oaxaca, Tlaxcala y Puebla*. Accessed April 15, 2024. https://cedocvirtual.sectur.gob.mx/janium/Documentos/12277.pdf.

Seligmann, Linda J. 2022. *Quinoa: Food Politics and Agrarian Life in the Andean Highlands*. Champaign: University of Illinois Press.

Serra Puche, Mari Carmen, and Jesús Carlos Lazcano Arce. 2012. "El mezcal en Xochitécatl-Cacaxtla, Tlaxcala." *Arqueología Mexicana* 19 (114): 44–51.

Signer, Rachel. 2016. "How the Mezcal Boom Is Threatening Wild Agave." *Punch*, June 16, 2016. https://punchdrink.com/articles/is-mezcals.

Silverstein, Michael. 2006. "Old Wine, New Ethnographic Lexicography." *Annual Review of Anthropology* 35:481–496.

Smith, Julia. 2018. "Coffee Landscapes, Specialty Coffee, Terroir, and Traceability in Costa Rica." *Culture, Agriculture, Food and Environment* 9. https://doi.org/10.1111/cuag.12103.

Sommers, Brian J. 2008. *The Geography of Wine: How Landscapes, Cultures, Terroir, and the Weather Make a Good Drop*. New York: Plume.

Stanford, Lois. 2012. "When the Marginal Becomes the Exotic: The Politics of Culinary Tourism in Indigenous Communities in Rural Mexico." In *Reimagining Marginalized Foods: Global Processes, Local Places*, edited by Elizabeth Finnis, 67–87. Tucson: University of Arizona Press.

Starkman, Alvin Gary. 2021. *Mezcal in the Global Spirits Market: Unrivaled Complexity, Innumerable Nuances*. Oaxaca, Mexico: Carteles Editores.

Stephen, Lynn. 2005. *Zapotec Women: Gender, Class, and Ethnicity in Globalized Oaxaca*. Durham, NC: Duke University Press.

Stephen, Lynn. 2007. *Transborder Lives: Indigenous Oaxacans in Mexico, California, and Oregon*. Durham, NC: Duke University Press.

Suddaby, Roy, Max Ganzin, and Alison Minkus. 2017. "Craft, Magic and the Re-Enchantment of the World." *European Management Journal* 35 (3): 285–296.

Taylor, Charles. 2003. *Modern Social Imaginaries*. Durham, NC: Duke University Press.

Taylor, Elise. 2018. "How Yola Jimenez Is Making Mezcal with Women's Empowerment in Mind." *Vogue*, February 27, 2018. https://www.vogue.com/article/yola-jimenez-yola-mezcal.

Taylor, Paul S. 1933. *A Spanish-Mexican Peasant Community: Arandas in Jalisco, Mexico*. Berkeley: University of California Press.

Taylor, William B. 1972. *Landlord and Peasant in Colonial Oaxaca*. Stanford, CA: Stanford University Press.

Taylor, William B. 1979. *Drinking, Homicide, and Rebellion in Colonial Mexican Villages*. Stanford, CA: Stanford University Press.

Terrazas, Francisco. 2017. "NOM-070-SCFI-2016: What Is in a Label?" *Mas Mezcal: Destination Unknown* (blog). October 10, 2017. https://www.masmezcal.com/mezcalvago/2017/10/2/nom-070-scfi-2016-what-is-in-a-label.

Toner, Deborah. 2015. *Alcohol and Nationhood in Nineteenth-Century Mexico*. Lincoln: University of Nebraska Press.

Toor, Frances. 1938. *Frances Toor's Motorist Guide to Mexico*. Mexico City: Frances Toor Studios.

Torrentera, Ulises. 2001. *Mezcalaria: cultura del mezcal*. Oaxaca, Mexico: Farolito Ediciones.

Torrentera, Ulises. 2009. *Breve guía del mezcal: historia del mezcal en síntesis*. Oaxaca, Mexico: Farolito Ediciones.

Torrentera, Ulises. 2017. *Miscella mezcalacea*. 2nd bilingual ed. Oaxaca, Mexico: Farolito Ediciones.

Transparency Market Research. 2019. *Mezcal Market Outlook, 2027*. Report, January 2019. https://www.transparencymarketresearch.com/mezcal-market.html.

Trubek, Amy B. 2009. *The Taste of Place: A Cultural Journey into Terroir*. Berkeley: University of California Press.

Tsing, Anna Lowenhaupt. 2015. *The Mushroom at the End of the World: On the Possibility of Life in Capitalist Ruins*. Princeton, NJ: Princeton University Press.

UNESCO (United Nations Educational, Scientific and Cultural Organization). n.d. "Agave Landscape and Ancient Industrial Facilities of Tequila." Accessed April 15, 2024. https://whc.unesco.org/en/list/1209.

US FDA (US Food and Drug Administration). 2023. "Del Maguey Issues Voluntary Recall of Promotional Ceramicware Cups Called 'Copitas' Used for Drinking Mezcal Because of Possible Health Risk." May 1, 2023. https://www.fda.gov/safety/recalls-market-withdrawals-safety-alerts/del-maguey-issues-voluntary-recall-promotional-ceramicware-cups-called-copitas-used-drinking-mezcal.

Valenzuela-Zapata, Ana G., and Gary Paul Nabhan. 2004. *Tequila: A Natural and Cultural History*. Tucson: University of Arizona Press.

Valles Septién, Carmen, ed. 1997. *Mezcal: Elixir de larga vida*. Mexico City: CVS Publicaciones.

Van den Berghe, Pierre L. 1994. *The Quest for the Other: Ethnic Tourism in San Cristobal, Mexico*. Seattle: University of Washington Press.

Vaughan, Mary Kay, and Stephen Lewis, eds. 2006. *The Eagle and the Virgin: Nation and Cultural Revolution in Mexico, 1920–1940*. Durham, NC: Duke University Press.

Vera Cortés, José Luis, and Rodolfo Fernández, eds. 2015. *Agua de las verdes matas: Tequila y mezcal*. Mexico City: Artes de Mexico y del Mundo.

Vive Oaxaca. 2014. "Lila Downs: Ven a Oaxaca ¡Tienes que vivirlo! (Promocional turístico)." YouTube video, 4:23, posted October 23, 2014. https://www.youtube.com/watch?v=KD8vb8noP84.

Vogel, Ann, and Alan Shipman. 2023. *Film Festivals and the Enrichment Economy: Cultural Value Chains in a Digital Media Age*. New York: Palgrave Macmillan.

Walker, Louise E. 2013. *Waking from the Dream: Mexico's Middle Classes after 1968*. Stanford, CA: Stanford University Press.

Wasserspring, Lois. 2000. *Oaxacan Ceramics: Traditional Folk Art by Oaxacan Women*. San Francisco: Chronicle Books.

Williams, Raymond. 1975. *The Country and the City*. Oxford: Oxford University Press.

Winters, Paul, and Benjamin Davis. 2009. "Designing a Programme to Support Smallholder Agriculture in Mexico: Lessons from PROCAMPO and *Oportunidades*." *Development Policy Review* 27 (5): 617–642.

Wood, W. Warner. 2008. *Made in Mexico: Zapotec Weavers and the Global Ethnic Art Market*. Bloomington: Indiana University Press.

Woods, Michael. 2007. "Engaging the Global Countryside: Globalization, Hybridity and the Reconstitution of Rural Place." *Process in Human Geography* 31 (4): 485–507.

Woods, Michael. 2018. "Precarious Rural Cosmopolitanism: Negotiating Globalization, Migration and Diversity in Irish Small Towns." *Journal of Rural Studies* 64:164–176.

Yola Mezcal. n.d. Home page. Accessed September 14, 2022. https://yolamezcal.com.

Index

Page numbers in *italics* refer to figures.

Kolibri 360 GmbH
Ferdinand-Jühlke-Straße 7
99095 Erfurt, Deutschland
produktsicherheit@kolibri360.de